The Music of American Folk Song
and Selected Other Writings on American Folk Music

Ruth Crawford Seeger, ca. 1949–50.

The Music of American Folk Song and Selected Other Writings on American Folk Music

Ruth Crawford Seeger

Edited by Larry Polansky
with Judith Tick

With a Historical Introduction by Judith Tick
and Forewords by Pete, Mike, and
Peggy Seeger

University of Rochester Press

First published 2001
by the University of Rochester Press

The University of Rochester Press is an imprint of Boydell & Brewer, Inc.
668 Mt. Hope Avenue, Rochester, NY 14620, USA
and of Boydell & Brewer, Ltd.
P.O. Box 9, Woodbridge, Suffolk IP12 3DF, UK

ISBN 1–58046–095–X
ISSN 1071–9989

Library of Congress Cataloging-in-Publication Data
Seeger, Ruth Crawford, 1901–1953.
  "The music of American folk song" and selected other writings on American folk music / Ruth Crawford Seeger ; edited by Larry Polansky with Judith Tick ; with a historical introduction by Judith Tick, and forewords by Pete, Mike, and Peggy Seeger.
    p. cm. — (Eastman studies in music ISSN 1071-9989 ; v. 17)
  Includes bibliographical references and index.
  ISBN 1-58046-095-X (alk. paper)
    1. Folk music—United States—History and criticism.   2. Musical notation.
  3. Oral tradition—United States.   4. Field recordings—History.   I. Polansky, Larry, 1954– .   II. Tick, Judith.   III.   IV. Eastman studies in music ; vol. 17.

ML3551.1.S44 2001
782.42162'13—dc21   2001035576

British Library Cataloguing-in-Publication Data
A catalogue record for this book is
available from the British Library

Designed and typeset by Straight Creek Bookmakers
Printed in the United States of America
This publication is printed on acid-free paper

Contents

The Music of American Folk Song
RUTH CRAWFORD SEEGER

Selected Other Writings on American Folk Music
Ruth Crawford Seeger

Illustrations

Music Examples

Figures in Editor's Endnotes

Appendix 3

Other Writings

Eastman Studies in Music

Ralph P. Locke, Senior Editor
Eastman School of Music

(ISSN 1071–9989)

Foreword

Pete Seeger

I was 11 or 12 when I first met Ruth Crawford, who became my stepmother a couple years later. She seemed to me the most honest person I had ever met in all my life.

One of my last memories of her was her leaning against a door jamb listening with me to a short piece of Japanese music which was especially eloquent because of its silences at various points.

The world lost a truly great musician when she died so young, so full of promise.

August 13, 1999

Foreword

A Few Personal Words about Ruth Crawford Seeger's *The Music of American Folk Song*

Mike Seeger

As I read my mother's introduction to *Our Singing Country* for the first time, it puts me to thinking about what was going on in my life at that time and its influence on my direction since. A lot of the core issues dealt with here seem both familiar and basic.

I was about seven years old as this introduction was being written. Both my mother and father had gotten me started singing ballads and songs such as *Barbara Allen* a couple of years earlier. The singing really took. Not so the piano.

I remember my first lesson well, when my mother sat me down at the piano and tried to get me started. I couldn't stand the idea of "practicing" and wouldn't do it. Perhaps I was already absorbing my parents' new devotion to traditional music and the informal ways that one can pick it up.

Also about the same time, either Charlie or Dio (childhood name for my mother) showed me how to operate the family record player that was used for transcribing all those field recordings. It was a black box with a hinged lid, and it was just large enough to have a variable-speed 12" turntable and about an 8" speaker. The needle that followed the grooves in the record could be removed by loosening a little thumbscrew, and there were two kinds of needles: a metal one that had to be replaced every few playings for commercial pressings, and a cactus one that played either commercial pressings or the aluminum field recordings that made up most of our family's recorded music collection. The cactus needle had to be sharpened after every playing of a side, or sound became dull or sometimes you'd play two grooves at the same time.

Our family collection consisted of a Wanda Landowska harpsichord record; a few commercial recordings of southern vernacular music such as Gid Tanner's Fiddler's Convention in Georgia (I almost wore it out); artists such as Sonny Boy Williamson, Fats Waller, Norman Phelps, Virginia Rounders, Billie Holiday (*Strange Fruit*), and Josh White; several off-center pressings of Ruth Crawford Seeger's *String Quartet, Andante*; and about 200 aluminum copies of field recordings by the Lomaxes, Sidney Robertson Cowell, Herbert Halpert, and my father. So I sat on the floor next to the piano playing those records and soaking up all that great music. I didn't play instruments except very basically on the autoharp; I just listened and sang the songs.

If I was stubborn about the piano and practicing, so was Dio persistent about her mission, the one so strongly expressed in *The Music of American Folk Song*. She wanted her children to appreciate this body of music and help carry it on. I'm sure she wanted me to try to play instrumental music. And she made what I think she probably thought of as her last try with me about ten years after she finished the *Our Singing Country* project.

When I graduated from high school she asked me if I'd like to take guitar lessons. I didn't like the idea of lessons but I did go along with it. I got on the bus and went downtown to take guitar lessons. For about three months my instructor was Charlie Byrd, who taught me a C chord and basic hand positions. He was gracious and easy-going and let me play approximately what was written in a book of scale exercises. The high point in my "studies" was an impromptu ten-minute jam session during one of my lessons, with Charlie and a country guitarist that happened to drop by. Now THAT was music education. Shortly after Charlie left the teaching staff, I quit the receiving end of formal music education and began learning traditionally the music that I had been hearing around home all my life.

I'm sure that our parents' response to the enduring musical, textual, and cultural value of traditional vernacular musics set my direction. Their radical feeling of mission from the 1930s became part of me. Many of us who remain engaged in and devoted to strictly traditional music are still discussing, learning, grappling with many of the issues that are dealt with in great detail and depth here. They are as interesting and timeless as the music itself.

My singing, my instrumental playing, my attitude towards the music, and my feeling of strong direction couldn't have happened any other way. As I read this introduction, written sixty years ago, I see what was a large part of how and why I got here.

December 2000

Foreword

Peggy Seeger

When I first read the last draft of Judith Tick's biography of my mother, I was in tears—tears of compassion and rage: compassion for my mother's battle to combine music and motherhood, and anger because she had died so very soon, before I had grown up enough to regard her as my comrade. She died when I was 18 and even had we known each other better at that time it is possible that my youth would have made complete understanding impossible. Children have a way of avoiding knowing their parents until they have gone from home or had children themselves. So now, at age 65, with a life behind me that much resembles my mother's as regards combining children with a creative musical talent, I have come to understand how difficult it must have been for her even to find time (much less concentration) to write this magnificent dissertation. In financial straits and with four children, she spent most of her time mothering and teaching piano. The transcribing was, of course, paid work—but I doubt that those who commissioned her to do that work counted on such a production as this. They probably wanted a simple reduction of the tune, a suggestion, a *soupçon*—that was the way things were (and are) done in most songbooks. They didn't know that Ruth Crawford Seeger was a perfectionist and that her main goal was to write down the tune exactly as she heard it.

Our house was run like a military campaign but it echoed with love, clean clothes, good food, freedom, and evenings of singing. Music was always playing somewhere in the house. Dio (as we called her) was always busy, always busy—and whether it was mending, cleaning the refrigerator out, or transcribing *Bad Bad Girl*, it was done meticulously. She'd put the needle down on the record, play a phrase and then lift it up again. Scribble something. Then the same line again. And again. And again. Scribble scribble. Very frustrating if you're six years old and want to hear the rest of the song. She'd sing *Groundhog* to us while we were running clothes through the old manual wringer or *Hanging Out the Linen Clothes* while pinning the sheets up on the big rack in the cellar. When Charlie (our father) came home at night, there would be supper, family time, and then music when we were in bed. They'd talk a lot about the work and then she'd play classical music on the piano.

This monograph, unedited, sat in my attic for 20 years awaiting my attention as editor. I never could have done it. It needed someone with a better understanding of the whole Ruth Crawford Seeger, the RCS that I did not confront until I read Judith Tick's superb book. But now—my anger has dispersed. After all, what do my children really know of me? Now, every publication, critique, recording or review that appears makes me glow, makes me wish so hard that she was here NOW—not only to see that she has at last been acclaimed as she deserved, but to know that I, for one, regard myself as her comrade.

Historical Introduction:
The Salvation of Writing Things Down

Judith Tick

This is a small book about small things. Sharps and flats, ties, dots and rests, flags added to note-heads here not there, movable bar lines, tiny curved lines called phrases, words altered by consonants added or subtracted, breaths taken in and let out later rather than sooner.

Making decisions about such small things occupied Ruth Crawford Seeger (1901–1953) from about 1937 to 1941, as she prepared transcriptions based on field recordings collected by John and Alan Lomax for their second American folk music anthology, *Our Singing Country* (1941).[1] As pioneering collectors of American folk music, the Lomaxes planned *Our Singing Country* as a sequel to their very successful *American Ballads and Folk Songs* (1934). Although the book did not sell as well as its predecessor (disappointing Alan Lomax in particular), *Our Singing Country* today commands indisputable stature in the literature of American traditional music. Crawford Seeger's superb craftsmanship in capturing what the composer Marc Blitzstein called "the alive musical moment" set standards for thoroughness and excellence which remain unsurpassed in twentieth-century anthologies devoted to this repertory. Blitzstein, who praised her "extraordinary precision and love," noted how the complexities of folk style held "no terrors for her."[2]

Blitzstein was right about the quality of her work, but wrong about the terrors. The more she listened, the more she heard. The more she heard, the greater the aesthetic challenge loomed about making the right choices. "She was just going to do the absolute best job possible—whatever it required," says Pete Seeger, witness to his stepmother's "fantastic determination." "I remember one week she was asking everybody to listen to a certain work song—some guy was hollering out in the fields and she said, 'Is that an A or an A sharp there?' And we'd listen to it and she knew she had to put down one or the other, and you know, what to do, what would be the best thing."[3] How to make clumsy Western-music notation express the intricacies of oral tradition? How to capture what Alan Lomax later described as its "ultimate originality"?[4] As Crawford Seeger traversed the minefields of African American spirituals, Caribbean part songs, cowboy ballads, Cajun lullabies, and Anglo-American fiddle tunes, a project which was supposed to take one year stretched into three. About 300 transcriptions later, when it came time to write her music editor's introduction for *Our Singing Country,* she produced *The Music of American Folk Song.*

The table of contents immediately shows the depth and range of her systematic investigation. Separate sections on "A Note on Transcription" and "Notes on the Songs and on Manners of Singing" are elaborated through precise scientifically articulated categories. Validating the idea of singing style as a worthy area of investigation, she documented every aspect of performance practice as fully as possible and then theorized her conclusions from the results. Concepts such as "majority usage" (Section 8) and "song norm" (Section 7) still retain their relevance. Fascinating case studies of multiple solutions to one transcription treat the level of detail as a negotiation between transcriber, singer, and new audience.

Crawford Seeger brought the powers of a composer to her project. Space here does not permit much recounting of her career as a pivotal figure in the post-Ives generation of American modernist composers, of her contemporary stature as an explorer of modern dissonance, or of the challenge such great works as her *String Quartet 1931* continue to pose. Small wonder, then, that *The Music of American Folk Song* allows us to hear American folk music through the ears of a composer and to appreciate musical nuances that might otherwise be missed. Of many cases in point I particularly relish the diagrams showing levels of transcription detail, moving from simple to complex in layers. As Crawford Seeger adds subtleties of pitch and rhythm to increasingly elaborate transcriptions for her illustration of options (as in the holler *Make Me a Garment,* Figure 8), we see through her x-ray ears to the inside of music-making.

Crawford Seeger intended *The Music of American Folk Song* to partner *Our Singing Country* as a long appendix. Perhaps a less idealistic person would have known from the start that such a visionary project, written in highly technical language—"an academic thesis" as the publishers described it—just might not get published as part of a commercial book. But Crawford Seeger, believing quite rightly that her treatment of American folk music was unique, assumed that the sheer originality of her work would jump over market hurdles. "She felt she'd have an argument, but she'd win," Pete Seeger recalled. [It was] "a big disappointment of the last ten years of her life. I was down in Washington when the Lomaxes said no and stood firm. She was very downcast for a while. I think she hoped she'd publish it some day."[5] Crawford Seeger was right about *The Music of American Folk Song*. It was unique then and it is unique now. Nothing else like it exists in the scholarly literature about American folk style.

How to make sense of the whole enterprise? As we explore its historical contexts, themes that shaped the century come into play: the link between nationalism and folk expression; the use of tradition as a wellspring for modernism; the transatlantic and transpacific interest in comparative musicology (or ethnomusicology, as it is now known).

Transcription loomed large in the early seminal work of pioneers in comparative musicology, such as Béla Bartók and the Hungarian émigré-scholar George Herzog. Crawford Seeger's work shares their intellectual intensity and accepts the profound responsibility they placed on the transcription process. In his posts at various American universities, Herzog had a major influence on the early priorities of comparative musicology. Crawford Seeger knew his work well, citing it in *The Music of American Folk Song*.[6] Here Charles Seeger 's early interest in the field—he was a co-founder of the pioneering American Society for Comparative Musicology—also played a part.[7] She "had read her Bartók and she had taken it very seriously, as she should," Alan Lomax said. "And she had read her Herzog; and she set out to make music look that way . . . and we went with her."[8] Their optimism drew on the energies of the moment, coalescing around the American urban folk revival movement.

The Music of American Folk Song stands at the threshold of the American urban folk revival movement in the late 1930s and 1940s— just at the time when folk music was being "discovered" by a middle-class urban public and coming into the consciousness of the country. We can only summarize briefly a historical narrative that many writers have shaped.[9] In the early decades of the century it was widely assumed that America had no folk music because it was a "mongrel" nation, where vestiges of old-country culture survived in isolation but nothing new of value was being created in this vast place that lacked pedigree. Such restrictive ideology was somewhat destabilized in the 1920s and 1930s through a variety of media, including race and hillbilly recordings and new folk song anthologies in print. Now the musics of the people deprecated by some in the scholarly establishment as "Niggah convicts and white bums" and the "underdog classes"—in short, the ethnic styles of the rural poor—were beginning their odyssey from the margins into the center of defining American identity.[10] By the end of the 1930s and early 1940s, in some important ways "regional" went "national," as folk music laid claim to the stature of an inclusive "American" legacy and the prestige of symbolic democratic art. In 1939 a famous modernist critic, Paul Rosenfeld, acknowledged the dynamic of conversion and the before-and-after that shaped the urban folk revival:

A sensitiveness to the American folksong . . . on the part of the members of the urban and "educated" public was an event of the most recent years. It was said that, unlike Russia, France and Germany, the United States possessed no folk music. That of the Negro was quite simply "African." That of the mountaineers—one had the word of earlier ballad-collectors—was entirely Anglo-Celtic. The emergence into full view of the American folksong, if not the main musical event of the present, is its main American-musical one.[11]

Among those who pushed "the emergence into full view of American folksong," Crawford Seeger and her New Deal colleagues deserve major credit. This story, so often told in terms of its great performers like Huddie Ledbetter and Woody Guthrie, unfolded through office-desk memos as well as purple-ditto-machined songsheets and through explicit cultural policy formulated by the White House. Decades later Alan Lomax stated it succinctly: "The revival really began under the New Deal in Washington. . . . They [the Roosevelts, the Hopkinses and the Tugwells] . . . saw that the country lacked a feeling of unity. They hoped that the cultivation of folk music, and the spread of the feeling of cultural unity that lies somehow embedded in our big and crazy patchwork of folksong, would give Americans the feeling that they all belonged to the same kind of culture."[12] In 1939, when the king and queen of England visited the Roosevelt White House, they heard Marian Anderson sing art songs and black spirituals, Alan Lomax play cowboy songs, and the Coon Creek Girls of Kentucky sing Southern mountain music.

In Washington, D. C., Crawford Seeger worked within an informal collective of New Deal activists, which in addition to her collaborator, Alan Lomax, included her husband, Charles Seeger, and their friend, the writer Benjamin Botkin. Empowered through federally funded cultural programs (such as the WPA Federal Writers Project and the Federal Music Project, the Joint Committee on Folk Arts, and the expanding Archive of American Folk Song at the Library of Congress), they provided ideological momentum and centralized projects of collection and documentation. As one historian has recently remarked, "they were creators as well as caretakers of a tradition."[13] Focusing on literature, Botkin argued for a dynamic view of folk expression as "functional" rather than antiquarian.[14] Charles Seeger jump-started American ethnomusicology from his analysis of folk-tune variants, and he reproached professional musicians (particularly teachers) for "deserting" American music.[15]

So much passion flowed from New Deal values into Crawford Seeger's work. She wrote *The Music of American Folk Song* as if she were writing a lawyer's brief for the Supreme Court of national cultural justice. She grappled with these questions: What constitutes American musical traditions in a multiethnic nation of immigrants? How do we experience (both appreciate and participate in) "folk culture" including folk art and folk music as living realities rather than antiquities? The more convention argued that folk song originated in some netherworld often labeled the "childhood of the race" and characterized its essence as "primitive" simplicity, the more she documented its complexity.[16] The more the music-appreciator movement touted classical music as the only kind of "good music," the more she celebrated the oppositional aspects of folk song practice. Her work acted as a gateway between past and present, creating different access points for multiple ways of hearing the old as new. Like Bartók, she admired oral tradition for the ways it flouted Romantic aesthetics. Just as he stressed the potential of Hungarian peasant music to counter the "excesses of Romanticists," so Crawford Seeger pointed to aspects of American folk music practice which were oppositional: where singing without dynamic variation seemed less manipulative (Section 4); where out-of-tuneness connected to the post-tonal ideas of obscure modernist theorists (see Section 28); where rhythms resisted regular meters.[17] Behind all of the detail lay an agenda of double proselytizing: to reach out to city people who could then embrace their lost heritage and to box the snobbish ears of Eurocentric professional musicians. While Alan Lomax framed the dialogue of transcription as a chance for "the country to come to town and teach town for a change,"[18] Crawford Seeger demonstrated how and why a "fine-art" reader might awaken to the "epic quality" of tradition (Section 4).

Just at the time Crawford Seeger was working on *The Music of American Folk Song,* she witnessed encouraging reactions from her composer colleagues. In 1939 the International Musicological Society, meeting in New York, sponsored concerts of Early American Folk-and-Art Music. It included performances by Alan Lomax, Aunt Molly Jackson, and the Nashville Old Harp Singers, who attracted the audience she hoped for. "Quite a few composers turned out with high enthusiasm for the day's orgy of American folk music," she wrote in a letter to a composer friend. "The excitement with which some of them greet this music is in itself exciting to us."[19] If those elite musicians could hear folk music as revelatory, then perhaps links between contemporary modernist music and vernacular expression might be forged through tradition. In the immediate years "some of them" included Virgil Thomson, Aaron Copland (who borrowed folk tunes from *Our Singing Country*), Kurt Weill, Roy Harris, and Samuel Barber. Sadly enough, Ruth Crawford Seeger did not compose much original music that realized her vision of ideal synthesis. With its quotations of three tunes from *Our Singing Country* (in particular, the fiddle tune *Callahan* mentioned in *The Music of American Folk Song*), her orchestral fantasy, *Rissolty Rossolty,* stands out as a successful but singular achievement in her small but choice body of work.

Yet *The Music of American Folk Song* and the work on *Our Singing Country* had a stunning impact within the Seeger family, whose multiple roles within many stages of the folk revival are widely acknowledged. Charles Seeger marked his wife's scholarly achievement as a turning point in his own intellectual development. He would develop, indeed appropriate in his later writings her language about singing style, performance practice, and transcription.[20] (His influential distinction between prescriptive and descriptive music has its roots here.) He in turn contributed his critical acumen to this project as well. Pete Seeger never forgot this manuscript, urging other family members to remember it as well, and encouraging the few who contemplated taking up its publication along the way. Over many decades for him this "appendix" has been worth remembering and worth reviving. Carriers of tradition, Mike Seeger and Peggy Seeger experienced the field recordings of *Our Singing Country* and their mother's involvement with *The Music of American Folk Song* as a formative time in their lives. With its publication readers who continue to feel reverberations of the folk revival's "excitement" about American musical tradition can appreciate the intellectual foundations of her achievement. Now they can, for the first time, fully greet not only the music Ruth Crawford Seeger so loved but her work in this field. It consolidates her achievement as one of the great composer-transcribers of the twentieth century.

Acknowledgments

Even if it took so many years to make this happen, this manuscript found its rightful editor and advocate in Larry Polansky, a composer who shares the dual orientation of its original author. Polansky knows Crawford Seeger's work from many perspectives. He has been inspired by her original music in his own compositions, and at the same time plays traditional music as part of his daily life. Perhaps most important, he matches what John Lomax once described as Crawford Seeger's "fanatical" concern for detail, reconstructing and annotating the text with scrupulousness and dedication. I have played a minor role in this project and wish to thank Larry Polansky for generously extending my "billing" to some public authorship. In addition, I am grateful to my husband, Stephen Oleskey, for his help and loving support.

Notes

1. John and Alan Lomax, eds., *Our Singing Country,* Ruth Crawford Seeger, music editor (1941, reprint, with a new introduction by Judith Tick, Mineola, N. Y.: Dover Publications, 2000).

2. Marc Blitzstein, "Singing Country," *Modern Music* 19 (Jan.-Feb. 1942): 139–40.

3. Interview of Pete Seeger by Mike Seeger, December 8, 1982 (Seeger Estate, quoted by permission).

4. Interview of Alan Lomax by Mike Seeger, January 5, 1983 (Seeger Estate).

5. Telephone interview of Pete Seeger by the author, November 21, 1990.

6. See the discussion of Herzog in Polansky's endnotes nos. vi and xv.

7. Ann M. Pescatello, *Charles Seeger: A Life in Music* (Pittsburgh: University of Pittsburgh Press, 1992), 123.

8. Comments by Lomax from an interview of Alan Lomax by Mike Seeger, January 6, 1983. Quoted in, Judith Tick, *Ruth Crawford Seeger: A Composer's Search for American Music* (Oxford: Oxford University Press, 1997), 410. For a discussion of transcription in ethnomusicology see Bruno Nettl, *The Study of Ethnomusicology* (Urbana: University of Illinois Press, 1983), chapter six.

9. See in particular, Norm Cohen, *Folk Song America: A 20th Century Revival* (Washington, D.C., Smithsonian Collection of Recordings, 1990) and Robert Cantwell, *When We Were Good: The Folk Revival* (Cambridge, Mass.: Harvard University Press, 1996).

10. Carl Engel in "Views and Reviews," *Musical Quarterly* 21 (1935): 108–9; Louise Pound, review of *Our Singing Country* in the *Journal of American Folklore* (Jan.-March 1943): 79–80.

11. Paul Rosenfeld, "Folksong and Culture-Politics," *Modern Music* 17 (Oct.-Nov. 1939): 20–22.

12. Alan Lomax, "Historical Origins of the Revival," in a symposium "The Folksong Revival," *New York Folklore Quarterly* 19/2 (April-June 1963): 121.

13. Benjamin Filene, "'Our Singing Country': John and Alan Lomax, Leadbelly, and the Construction of an American Past," *American Quarterly* 43 (December 1991): 604–24.

14. On Botkin see Jerrold Hirsch, "Folklore in the Making, B. A. Botkin," *Journal of American Folklore* 100 (1987): 3–38.

15. "American music, deserted by professional musicians, has made music from its own soil and from the common people, from whom we have the old folk songs, the Negro songs, the hillbilly songs, and the cowboy songs. Composers, critics, historians, in fact all but teachers, have come to recognize American music," from a speech made to teachers of the Florida Music Project in Jacksonville in 1939, as cited in Pescatello, *Charles Seeger,* p. 156.

16. For a fuller discussion of these ideas see Tick, *Ruth Crawford Seeger,* chapter 16.

17. Béla Bartók, "The Influence of Peasant Music on Modern Music" (1931) reprinted in his *Essays,* ed. Benjamin Suchoff (New York: St. Martin's Press, 1976), 340–44.

18. Alan Lomax, "Revealing the People's Art," remarks in the symposium "The Folksong Revival," 127.

19. Letter from Ruth Crawford Seeger to John Becker, Sept. 22, 1939 (Seeger Estate).

20. I discuss this in detail in "Ruth Crawford, Charles Seeger, and *The Music of American Folk Songs,*" in *Understanding Charles Seeger, Pioneer in American Musicology,* ed. Bell Yung and Helen Rees (Urbana: University of Illinois Press, 1999), 109–29.

Editor's Introduction

Larry Polansky

Habent sua fata libelli
("Books have their own destiny")
—*Béla Bartók*

This edition makes available, for the first time, Ruth Crawford Seeger's most visionary, detailed, and complex writing on American folk music. Entitled *The Music of American Folk Song,* this monograph was originally intended as an "Appendix" or "Introduction" for one of the finest collections of American folk song ever assembled, *Our Singing Country* (1941) (*OSC*), by John and Alan Lomax, with transcriptions by Ruth Crawford Seeger.

Ruth Crawford Seeger (RCS) scholars have documented the history and provenance of this monograph: its painstaking, demanding writing, editing, and eventual agonized and controversial demotion to a short "Music Preface," which appeared in *Our Singing Country.* The most complete history is found in Judith Tick's recent biography of RCS. Matilda Gaume's early biography and a little known but pioneering master's thesis by Karen Cardullo are also important sources on the monograph.[1]

The monograph's existence has been known to a few scholars for some thirty years, as well as to members of the Seeger family, who have long understood its importance for American folk music scholarship. Partially incomplete, unedited, somewhat scrambled, and missing some examples, it became a formidable and time-consuming—yet extremely rewarding—task to reconstruct and publish. RCS was "discovered" first by the contemporary "art" music community, so it is perhaps logical that her compositional work was dealt with before her folk music scholarship. In addition, most of her work on folk song *had* been published, in the three books of folk songs for children² and in various other projects. There seemed, perhaps, less need to resurrect a difficult, technical, and rarified philosophical manuscript which had, in fact, been published (in drastically reduced form) as the Music Preface to *OSC*. Like Melville's *Billy Budd, The Music of American Folk Song* sat in a few well-placed drawers, known to just a few people. And as with Melville's posthumously published masterpiece, RCS's *The Music of American Folk Song* will come to be known as one of her most brilliant achievements.

Reading this monograph while listening to the original recordings (many of which are available on long-playing records and compact discs) is a rewarding experience. Following RCS's transcriptions, and reading her explanations, the reader/listener gets a sense of the extraordinary challenge she faced. Complicated written descriptions of minute decision-making procedures become resonant musical insights when listening to the tunes themselves. It is fascinating to imagine her task—responsibly transcribing these songs for the first time, for a reading public which would have little or no other experience with this music. Her transcriptions were to become the way a nation would *see* its folk music. (The Lomaxes referred to some of their early 1930s recordings as "sound photographs."³) Ideas about intonation, interstanzaic variation, model and initial tunes become far more practical and less theoretical as sound becomes page.

There were few precedents for *The Music of American Folk Song* in American music scholarship. RCS took existing field recordings and transcribed, in her own words, the "breath of the singer." Though the early work of scholars and folk song collectors like George Herzog and Bela Bartók influenced her, their more intellectually enlightened notions of folk song scholarship had yet to become integrated in any but a few publications. As Cardullo points out, American folk song scholarship in the late 1930s was undergoing a revolution in ideology and practice, but RCS's work was a radical effort in terms of the degree to which it attempted to capture, as fully as possible, and with tremendous respect, complex musical ideas within the frustrating constraints of western notation. As transcriber/scholar, she was pretty much forced to devise her own rules and methodology for taking this important next step in the understanding of our musical traditions. In taking that step, she prepared succeeding generations of "scholar/artists" to go beyond recording and transcription, and learn to play the music themselves.

Most earlier collections, dating back, of course, to the nineteenth century, represented various attempts not only to transcribe the music but to translate (and usually simplify) it to a more "civilized" sensibility. RCS instinctively gravitated toward the musical complexity and richness of the material in an unusual way. Her association with Charles Seeger, Benjamin Botkin, and the Lomaxes, and her generally forward-looking and uncompromising views on music itself, convinced her that this music was, in and of itself, complete. There was no need for refinement, apology, translation, or simplification. It *was* in need of careful explication, energetic advocacy, and unbiased transcription. One can almost imagine RCS saying to herself, reading earlier transcribers' work: "A 5/4 is a 5/4, and should be written as such!"

Although her approach may now seem less remarkable, it represented an enormous change and risk for RCS and the Lomaxes. In the 1930s, RCS "discovered" American folk music. In *OSC* and *The Music of American Folk Song* she takes a major step forward. As Bluestein points out, "[in *OSC*] earlier apologies for the dearth or inferiority of American songs were replaced by a full-throated declaration of musical independence."[4] Her work for *OSC* contains no remnants of the romantic pondering the primitive. She finds folk song as difficult to explicate as a Webern string quartet. Like Béla Bartók, that other great composer/transcriber, she could not, and *would* not, in good faith, intellectually *allow* for the possibility of any musical idiom being aesthetically inferior to, or less sophisticated than any other.

Anthony Seeger, in his review of Tick's biography, describes the synergy of RCS as composer/transcriber/scholar:

> The description of Ruth's collaboration with the Lomaxes, and her agonies trying to accurately transcribe "folk music," should interest many ethnomusicologists at a time when transcription is out of vogue. Reading about her agonies over a small phrase one might wonder why an avant-garde composer would spend so much time transcribing Library of Congress recordings of rural musicians, when less time would earn as much money. In fact I think Tick is correct: only a very fine and experimental musician could both recognize and appreciate what those artists were doing musically. Ruth, listening with tremendous concentration and intuition, understood that the musicians whom she was transcribing were not necessarily doing something simple because they were

"simple folk.". . . The feeling of affiliation between the avant-garde and the vernacular arts is found in many places, and cannot be reduced to exoticism and exploitation. It is partly the result of intellectual openness and appreciation of craft. Ruth Crawford never stopped being an avant-garde composer, but she used her skills in a different way with the Library of Congress recordings. She also believed her transcriptions were her art. . . .[5]

Musical sophistication had been taken from American folk musicians by the musical sophisticates who had transcribed their songs. Ruth Crawford Seeger, in *Our Singing Country,* in what Tick has called an "act of will," was determined to return that sophistication to them. As a composer of difficult and visionary music, she understood that musical ideas, no matter how unusual for the general public, could and should remain in their purest, truest form. *The Music of American Folk Song* is a crucial "missing link" not only in our knowledge of her musical life, but in the history of American folk music.

RCS's approach to this music is almost completely devoid of cultural assumptions and questions of race and ethnicity. Perhaps because she worked completely from recordings, she focused on the sonic artifacts of what have come to be regarded in recent ethnomusicological thought as problematic social, political, and racial interactions. Her tremendous love and respect for *the music itself* allowed her to assume a benign cultural stance. The implicit cultural difficulties about which, for example, Hirsch writes with respect to John Lomax's relationship with African American singers,[6] is noticeably absent in her careful, always musically motivated, discussions of the "singer and the song."

Like RCS, I am a composer, primarily interested in *the work itself*. This manuscript has been unpublished for some sixty years. My intention in this edition is similar to RCS's with regard to the songs of OSC—to present and clarify, not explain or analyze.

Main Sources Used

1. Manuscript Sources

The earlier, fairly complete typescript entitled "Appendix," located in the Library of Congress. Abbreviated in this edition α (Alpha)

The later, foundational typescript called "The Music of American Folk Song," in the possession of the Seeger Family. Abbreviated **β** (Beta)

Miscellaneous, out of order, probably intermediary pages (between α and β) included at the end of an existing copy of β, in the possession of the Seeger family. Abbreviated **β-m**

Manuscript pages for "1001 Folksongs," an uncompleted project, by RCS with Duncan Emrich and Charles Seeger, still in manuscript. In the possession of the Seeger family. This was a source for several alternate transcriptions of songs mentioned in this edition. Abbreviated **"1001 Folksongs" Papers**

Collection of early, incomplete, marked up and pasted together sources for early drafts and notes, included in the Library of Congress Ruth Crawford Seeger collection (Item 47). Abbreviated **LC47**

These sources have several titles including "Music Introduction" and "Appendix to the Music." LC47 includes other handwritten pages, examples, and charts (including a hand-redrawn set of charts of the Metfessel *Swing Low . . .* figures). α is also in LC47, and since these materials are available at the Library of Congress, α has, until now, been a source for others reading this document. Since α is more complete than the other materials in LC47, it is referred to individually in this edition.

Lomax (John Avery) Family Papers, in the Center for American History, University of Texas at Austin. These papers contain drafts for the Lomax introductions to *OSC,* over 30 unpublished transcriptions by RCS intended for *OSC,* and a number of other materials relevant to this monograph. Abbreviated **Lomax Family Papers**

2. Published Sources Frequently Referred to in This Edition

a. About "Our Singing Country" and Ruth Crawford Seeger

Ruth Crawford Seeger. The "Music Preface" published in *Our Singing Country.* Abbreviated **"Music Preface"** to *OSC*

John and Alan Lomax, eds. *Our Singing Country.* Ruth Crawford Seeger, Music Editor. New York: Macmillan, 1941. Reprint, with a new introduction by Judith Tick. Mineola, N.Y.: Dover, 2000. Abbreviated **OSC**

Judith Tick. *Ruth Crawford Seeger: A Composer's Search for American Music.* New York: Oxford University Press, 1997. Abbreviated **Tick**

The authoritative biography of RCS. Chapters 16 and 17 deal extensively with *OSC,* and provide a complementary history and critical analysis to this edition. References to Tick's other writings are cited specifically.

Matilda Gaume. *Ruth Crawford Seeger: Memoirs, Memories, Music.* Metuchen, N.J.: Scarecrow Press, 1986. Abbreviated **Gaume**
The first biography of RCS.

Karen Mandeville Cardullo. "Ruth Crawford Seeger: Preserver of American Folk Music." Master's Thesis, George Washington University, 1980. Abbreviated **Cardullo**
This thesis contains an excellent summary of the monograph.

b. About the Songs in the Archive of American Folk Song

Charles Seeger's *Check-List of Recorded Songs in the English Language in the Archive of American Folk Song to July, 1940.* Washington, D.C.: Music Division, The Library of Congress, 1942; and the addendum "Supplementary Listing of Recorded Songs in the English Language in the Library of Congress Archive of Folk Song through Recording No. AFS 4332 (October, 1940)." Compiled by Deborah Deems and William Nowlin for the Archive of American Folk Song. Washington, D.C.: Library of Congress, June 13, 1977. Abbreviated **Charles Seeger,** *Check-List*

Library of Congress, American Folklife Center, Archive of American Folk Song.
In *Our Singing Country* (and in most other sources), songs (recordings) are listed with their AFS recording number, referring to the Library of Congress American Folklife Center catalog which contains thousands of recording citations.

Library of Congress LP Record Series of songs from the Archive of American Folk Song collection. LPs are referred to by their number. For example, AFS L2 is *Anglo-American Shanties, Lyric Songs, Dance Tunes and Spirituals.*
Many of these songs are also available on CD (on Rounder) and are co-referenced in this edition by their Rounder CD number, generally in the low 1500s. (See the document "Folk Recordings, Selected from the Archive of Folk Culture," Washington, D.C., Library of Congress, 1989.) Abbreviated **AFS L[ ]** and **Rounder 151[ ]**

A Treasury of Library of Congress Field Recordings. Selected and Annotated by Stephen Wade. Rounder 1500 CD. Abbreviated **Rounder** *Treasury*

The *Deep River of Song* (The Alan Lomax Collection) anthology on
  Rounder records. Abbreviated **Rounder 1821–27**
    Songs on these CDs are referred to by a numerical shorthand
for their CD number. For example, the CD *Black Texicans* is
Rounder 1821. These CDs are:

11661–1821–2	*Black Texicans*
11661–1822–2	*Bahamas 1935*
11661–1823–2	*Black Appalachia*
11661–1824–2	*Mississippi: Saints and Sinners*
11661–1826–2	*Big Brazos*
11661–1827–2	*Virginia and the Piedmont*

and (not part of the *Deep River . . .* series)

11661–1842–2	*Cajun & Creole Music 1934/1937*
11661–1843–2	*Cajun & Creole Music II 1934/1937*

These recordings are still being released. Other songs mentioned
in this edition are likely to become commercially available in the
near future.

Provenance

There are four primary manuscript and typescript sources for this
edition. In what I believe is their chronological order, they are: LC47,
α, β-m, and β (see list of sources above).

  The writing of *The Music of American Folk Song* occupied several years of RCS's life in the late 1930s and 1940–41, during which
she made several nearly complete versions. She referred to the monograph, more or less chronologically, as the "Music Introduction" (or
just "Introduction"), the "Appendix," and finally, "The Music of
American Folk Song(s)."

  The collection of earlier materials I call LC47 is grouped together
in the Library of Congress under that item number. They are incomplete, short, and do not contain examples. They do, however, contain handwritten notes and sketches for examples which have occasionally been integrated into this edition. LC47 was not a direct source
for this edition's reconstruction, but was used to clarify problematic
passages and to complete the edition from the point where β stops
before the end of the monograph.

  The writing sequence seems to have been (post-LC47):

1) α: first draft (with almost no figures)
2) β-m: selectively rewritten second draft, of certain sections, passages, and pages
3) β: second draft, intended to be nearly final, with many figures and pencil revisions. β is incomplete: several pages are missing in the beginning, and it ends about 4/5ths of the way through.

α is available in the Library of Congress. β-m is an intermediary collection of extra pages, examples, and rewritten passages. β is the closest to an "ur" typescript. β and β-m have been in the possession of the Seeger family and have been referred to by several scholars. For example, page number references in Cardullo refer to β. This edition proceeds from the assumption that RCS never completed this monograph. Some of the material in β (and, in fact, α) appeared in the published "Music Preface" to *OSC,* but was significantly condensed, with most of the theoretical and philosophical content deleted. The editor's endnotes in this publication indicate a few places where material in *The Music of American Folk Song* became part of the "Music Preface." In addition, some examples in this edition (concerning rhythmic notation) appear in the "Music Preface," but were never inserted into β.

There are many intricate editorial pencil indications in α, as well as references to the "Music Preface," suggesting that this was, at least initially, intended as a kind of draft for publication. There is evidence also that, at some stage of its writing, RCS realized that *The Music of American Folk Song* would have to be abandoned in favor of what would become the "Music Preface." β might thus be very late (1940, or even 1941?).[7]

For this edition, β and β-m are used until near the end, at which point α is used to complete the monograph. The editor's endnotes document the sources of sections, passages, sentences, sometimes even words. Unless otherwise noted the text is from β. There are many fewer music examples in α; this partially explains why, in this edition, they stop around Section 26, where β ends. α, however, contains several song citations not in β.[8] Most of the sections that follow Section 24a come from α and β-m, and most of the preceding sections from β. The writing in α is less robust, sometimes shorter, and not as fully edited.

Even in β, the writing was never subjected to the iterative editorial process usually necessary for publication. It is less polished than RCS's other published prose. This edition consists of what would have been at least one draft prior to the one that would have been submitted to Macmillan's editors, had this monograph been published in *OCS*. Considering that it never existed in more than draft form, it is beautifully written. It has the kind of keen, almost alarming intelligence and clarity associated with her writing and music.

The following two excerpts—the same passage in α and β respectively—exemplify the gradient of edition between the two sources:

α: Any study of relative phrase-lengths should be made on the basis of consideration of all stanzas of the song, since in some stanzas the singer may add, and in others, subtract a full measure or more. In this collection well over half of the songs, as sung through from beginning to end, exhibit a four-measure phrase-pattern, the length of the measure being sometimes modified by prolonging or contracting of beats within them. [After this, one half-paragraph follows, which is crossed out.]

β: Obviously, any comprehensive study of phrase-lengths should be made upon the basis of acquaintance with all stanzas of the song, since any one phrase, recurrent from stanza to stanza throughout the song, may show interstanzaic variation in length.

The endnotes include a number of comparisons between the language of α and β.

Technical Conventions

- The musical examples, most in RCS's hand in the sources, have been typeset for this edition. A number of very minor changes have been made in autography, and a number of obvious minor errors corrected. There are several sources for the musical examples (manuscript sources and *OSC*), and when not directly from β the source is indicated in the endnotes.
- Footnotes are RCS's, as they appear in the typescript. All endnotes to the monograph are mine. Because of the reconstruction process, footnote numbers in this edition, especially towards the end, do not correspond exactly to the sources. Editor's endnotes to RCS's writings are numbered with roman

numerals; endnotes to the editors' writings are numbered in
arabic numerals.

- There are pencil indications, cross-outs, and other editorial
  emendations in the typescripts. Most of these are, presumably,
  by RCS, but some are probably made by others (Charles Seeger
  or later scholars). In many cases the endnotes indicate where
  these notations occur and the specific textual choice made for
  this edition. In a few cases the editorial decision was so minor
  that, for the sake of brevity, no mention is made of it.

- Song titles are spelled in this edition as they appear in the index
  in *OSC*, often differing from the spelling in the sources. Even
  within the sources, the same song may have different spellings
  (probably changed over time). Most spelling differences between
  OSC and the sources are minor, involving the omission of articles or hyphens, or involving slight vowel changes. Appendix
  1 contains a list of songs mentioned in the edition, with spelling
  differences in *OSC*. Obviously, in folk music sources besides
  OSC, there are many variant titles and spellings (not to mention versions) of these songs. In this edition variants are usually
  (but not always) irrelevant, since all song references are to specific recordings in the Archive of American Folk Song at the
  Library of Congress.

- Song titles, usually underlined in the typescripts, are italicized
  in this edition. Although this is unusual in modern usage, it
  respects what I believe to be a strongly felt pencilled note in α
  (on one of the multiple first pages, in the top right hand corner): "Place song titles in italics not double quotes." In *OSC*
  song titles appear in quotes (in the Preface and Introduction),
  following common practice for the time. I believe that RCS felt
  the songs to be of italics-level significance (like composition
  titles). In this edition, her mandate is followed. A curious exception is the song *The "Bigler"* (the spelling used in this edition), partially italicized in *OSC* because of the proper name (a
  schooner). Italicizing song titles creates an unusual typographical problem in lists (as in *Ol' Hannah*; *You Kicked and Stomped
  and Beat Me*; *Look Down That Lonesome Road*; *Dupree*; *I've
  Been a Bad, Bad Girl*; *John Riley*)—titles with internal commas
  are occasionally difficult to parse (*Mamma, Mamma, Make Me
  a Garment*). The reader, when confused, is referred to Appendix 1.

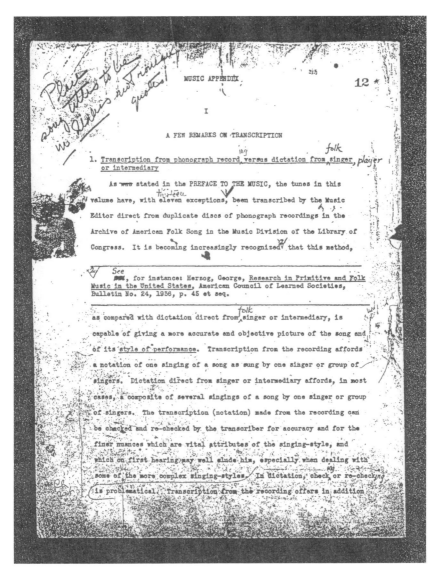

Plate 1. First page of β ("A Few Remarks on Transcription"), showing Ruth Crawford Seeger's handwritten note: "Place song titles in Italics not double quotes." (Photo, Library of Congress. Used by permission.)

- An occasional spelling or punctuation has been slightly updated or standardized without comment, especially in cases that could lead to misunderstanding or to awkwardness in reading today.
- No attempt is made to modernize problematic language. RCS uses the word "Negro" and gender-specific pronouns. Songs in *OSC* contain far more offensive language. RCS, with her deeply humanistic, careful, inventive feeling for language, would have almost certainly been sympathetic to minor alterations in order to update the language to contemporary standards. Although I considered doing so, I have decided, in the end, to leave the language as it is, and hope that the reader will understand this difficult editorial decision.
- Square brackets [ ] indicate an editorial emendation or missing text.

The Title

The intended title of this monograph is still in some doubt. It was variously called (by RCS in her writings, and other scholars since) the "Appendix," "Introduction," "Music Introduction," and finally, the "Preface" to OSC. The title chosen for this edition, *The Music of American Folk Song*, differs from the ones used by Cardullo, Tick, Gaume, and other scholars. The variables are the introductory article ("Music of American Folk Songs") and whether "Folk Song" is one word or two, and/or plural.[9]

There are a number of title pages in the sources. The one that seems definitive (in β) has a number of pencil indications:

~~THE~~ [The] MUSIC OF ~~SOME~~ AMERICAN FOLK SONG~~S~~

by
Ruth Crawford Seeger

~~A Music~~ Appendix to the ~~music of~~
OUR SINGING COUNTRY

by
John A and Alan Lomax
and
Ruth Crawford Seeger,

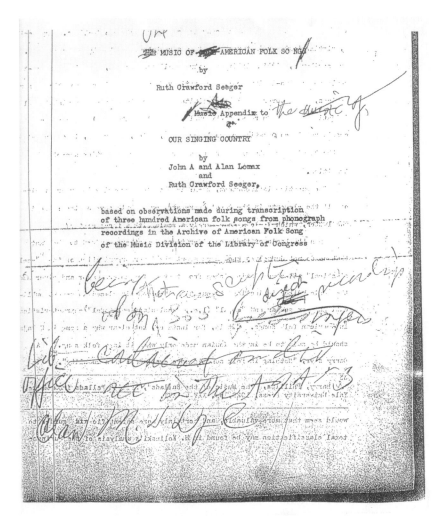

Plate 2. Title page from β, showing title changes and markings. (Photo, Seeger family. Used by permission.)

In the first line, the first word "THE" is crossed out, and written in again, above, in pencil. The word "SOME" is crossed out heavily, and the final "S" on "SONGS" is also crossed out heavily. It thus reads "The Music of American Folk Song" (our title). On the fourth line, the words "A Music" are crossed out, the words "the music of" are written in pencil, and the two words "music of" are crossed out, appearing as "Appendix to the OUR SINGING COUNTRY." The word "the" after "Appendix to" was probably meant to be crossed out as well.

This page appears to be the most recent, although it is difficult to be certain. There is reason to believe that RCS wanted the title "folk song" to correspond in usage to the name of the institution (Archive of American Folk Song) which was the music's home.

An earlier draft of this title page (in LC47) reads:

THE MUSIC OF SOME AMERICAN FOLK SONGS
as observed during transcription

There are some other versions (final "s" not crossed out, and other variants).

The change, in RCS's own drafts, from "Introduction" to "Appendix" has been confusing to various writers. It may not be significant. The monograph was never intended, in any case, as simply a "Preface." It became the latter because of the differences between RCS and the Lomaxes and publisher, and because of its length and difficulty. The reduction to "Music Preface" occurred late and under severe time constraints.[10]

A Few Remarks on the Songs

When RCS made these transcriptions, and wrote *The Music of American Folk Song,* the recordings of these songs had not yet been publicly released. The Library of Congress decided to do this in 1941.[11] RCS's transcriptions, when she made them, were the *only* way that these songs were *described* for the public. She noted that nothing would replace the experience of listening to them, but in 1939–41, that opportunity was available to only a few fortunate musicians and scholars. As such, her transcriptions functioned, to some extent, as recordings do now.[12]

To assist the reader in listening to the songs while reading about them, commercial releases of recordings from the Archive of American Folk Song are cited in the endnotes the first time the corresponding song is mentioned in the monograph. These citations are not exhaustive—there have been a great many releases, authorized and not, on many labels (defunct and not) of this material. The citations focus on the Rounder and Library of Congress series, since these discs use primary materials and are made with the cooperation of the Lomax Archives and the Archive of American Folk Song at the American Folklife Center of the Library of Congress.

About 300 songs were transcribed for *OSC*; 205 were published. Appendix 1 contains a list of the 147 songs mentioned in this monograph, with variant spellings from *OSC*. Appendix 2 lists 34 transcriptions found in the Lomax Family Papers.

In Charles Seeger's *Check-List*, many of the songs have slightly variant names, and derive from common archetypes. For example, *The Low-down, Lonesome Low* [OSC] is listed in the *Check-List* as *The Low and Lonesome Low*, and is one of a large group of songs known commonly as variants of the Child ballad *The Golden Vanity*.

The following songs are mentioned in this edition but not included in *OSC*:

The Buffalo Skinners
Drop 'em Down (cited by RCS in β as not included in *OSC*)
Au Long de ce Rivage (only mentioned in α)
The Raving Shanty Boy (only mentioned in α)
Washington the Great (only mentioned in α)

Except for *The Buffalo Skinners*, these songs were probably transcribed from the recordings, but not selected for inclusion (there are, in fact, extant transcriptions for *Drop 'em Down*). All but one (*Au Long de ce Rivage*) are listed in Charles Seeger's *Check-List* (which contains only English songs). Other songs are mentioned in α and LC47, occurring in sections superceded by β, and as such are not integrated into this edition.

There are many cognate songs on the Rounder and Library of Congress collections, but only a few of the actual recordings released so far are the ones transcribed for *OSC*. For example, a version of *John Henry* exists on Rounder 1823, but it is not the one in *OSC*.

Plate 3. Ruth Crawford Seeger's sketch for her transcription of *Drop 'em Down*. (Photo, Lomax [John Avery] Family Papers, Center for American History, University of Texas at Austin. Used by permission.)

The Rounder Alan Lomax Collection is drawn from recordings in the Lomax Archives, not the Library of Congress. However, there are many duplicate disks in the two collections, so many of these recordings are those used in *OSC*.

Besides Charles Seeger's *Check-List,* written around the time of RCS's monograph, other important resources for locating songs and recordings are:

Bartis, Peter. "A History of the Archive of Folk Song at the Library of Congress: The First Fifty Years." Ph.D. Dissertation, University of Pennsylvania, 1982.

Bean, Charles W. "An Index of Folksongs Contained in Theses and Dissertations in the Library of Congress." Master's Thesis, Dept. of Library and Information Studies, Loughborough University of Technology, Loughborough, Leicestershire, England, October 1981.

Brunnings, Florence. *Folk Song Index: A Comprehensive Guide to the Florence E. Brunnings Collection.* New York: Garland, 1981.
   This is an invaluable cross-listing of recordings, singers, books, and resources.

Cutting, Jennifer, ed. "American Folk Music and Folklore Recordings: A Selected List." Washington, D.C.: American Folklife Center, Library of Congress, Annual.

"Finding and Reference Aids Prepared for the Archive of Folk Culture." Washington, D.C.: The American Folklife Center, Library of Congress, 1997 (revised periodically).

Folk Music: A Catalog of Folk Songs, Ballads, Dances, Instrumental Pieces, and Folk Tales of the United States and Latin America on Phonograph Records. Washington, D.C.: Music Division, Recording Laboratory, Reference Department, Library of Congress, 1964.

Folk Recordings, Selected from the Archive of Folk Culture. Washington, D.C.: Motion Picture, Broadcasting and Recorded Sound Division, Library of Congress, 1989.

A Note on the Notes

All endnotes to the text of *The Music of American Folk Song* are mine. Each is specifically motivated by RCS's text. They are intended to provide amplifications, references, and technical explanations regarding manuscript reconstruction and editing. As a composer and musician myself, with a lifelong passion for American folk music, I have taken the liberty of including a few personal and musical observations, in addition to many small explanations and contextualizations for RCS's writing. My intention is to make the edition self-contained for the non-specialized reader and to provide assistance to all levels and variety of readership. In all cases, I have tried to write "alongside" the text rather than "about" it.

All footnotes are by RCS from the original sources. Their format has been changed to reflect current (*Chicago Manual of Style*) standards. An occasional element of the citation has been added without comment.

Acknowledgments

When this project was first suggested to me by Judith Tick and members of the Seeger family (Mike, Peggy, and Pete), I had little idea of its scope, or that it would occupy my ears, mind, and life for such a long time. Like *The Music of American Folk Song* itself, "a project scheduled to take one summer stretched into three years."[13] A simple editing project became a major reconstructive and research effort.

First of all, I would like to thank the family of RCS and the executors of her estate for permission to use materials in their possession or under their jurisdiction, as well as those in the Library of Congress.

I am grateful to and honored by the Parsons Fund of the American Folklife Center for supporting my work on this edition with a Parsons Fellowship.

One of the nicest things about working on this edition was the opportunity to meet a number of people whom, as a composer, I might not have ordinarily been lucky enough to meet. Karen Cardullo, who graciously gave of her time in talking to me, shared her early work on RCS's folk song scholarship, as well as her infectious enthusiasm. Judith Gray, James Hardin, Jennifer Cutting, Joe Hickerson, and Ann Hoog (who served as a second pair of ears for a number of songs), of the American Folklife Center, were the most knowledgeable, able, hospitable, and above all, fun hosts one could imagine during my week of work there. Ruth Voss and Robin Rausch of the Performing Arts Reading Room at the Library of Congress, were also helpful to my work. John Wheat at the University of Texas at Austin, Center for American History Archive, was helpful in locating some of the "missing" transcriptions.

The music librarians at the Paddock Music Library at Dartmouth College were indispensable and energetic on my behalf. Special Librarian Helmut Baer was indefatigable in helping me find obscure materials. Librarians Patricia Fisken, Patricia Morris, and the rest of the staff, as usual, made working there a great pleasure and immensely productive. Dartmouth College colleague Steve Swayne helped with an important detail. The college itself, my employer for about a decade now, has continued to provide a supportive environment for my work.

Several musician friends were kind enough to read the manuscript and offer invaluable editorial comments. Composer Eric Richards pointed out, and I agree, that *The Music of American Folk Song* is the composition textbook RCS never wrote, and is invaluable to us composers. Mary Ann Haagen made a number of very important comments and suggestions, and discussed several ideas about folk music with me at great length. In addition, through her work with Shaker music and the Enfield Shaker Singers, she has, for the past few years, provided me (and my family) with a wonderful alternative to writing about folk music (that is, singing it).

David Fuqua computer-typeset the musical examples, and once again, I am grateful for his hard work and extraordinary knowledge of musical notation. He contributed a number of important editorial suggestions as well.

To Ralph P. Locke, senior editor of Eastman Studies in Music; to Molly Cort and Tim Madigan of the University of Rochester Press; and to copyeditor Louise Goldberg, my deepest appreciation for all their hard work and intelligence and for making this book possible.

Ruth Crawford Seeger herself can help conclude these acknowledgments, in an excerpt from her poignant epistolary autobiographical "Letter to Miss Prink":

All this time, remember your editor in New York, Miss Prink. Also the songs you promised to send her "in a day or two." Also remember the footnotes, which have received considerable change due to the last few weeks' work on the manuscript. Dread her reaction to this. Therefore, decide to postpone sending them a day or two more. Also, remember there are a few more all night sessions due on the Appendix. Remember further that the Appendix is materially longer than Miss Prink anticipates. Try to decide how, without seeming vain, you can indicate to her that, this Appendix being unique as a musical treatment of American folk music, it must go through uncut. Also, recall that you do not wish to release it until you have gone over it with your husband. This will remind you that he is in the midst of writing several papers for various meetings of various societies, plus music editing a book himself, all aside from his full time duties in the town. Ponder this dilemma while hanging out the 42 socks and the 21 shorts and delicacies; also while squeezing the oranges for orange juice, admiring Peggy's mass production of pictures on your favorite onion-skin paper (due for carbon copies of the Appendix), giving Barbara (upstairs) more blocks, and suggesting to Michael (upstairs) that he cover his bed with only a portion of his toys.

I would like to thank my own "Miss Prinks"—Mike, Peggy, and Pete Seeger, and Alexia Smith—who gave me a singular honor: the opportunity to work on this project. They have been generous with their time and interest, and have inspired me in ways both musical and personal. My friend and co-editor Judith Tick has been patient with my sometimes glacial progress, and she claims to be grateful for what she refers to as my "obsessive Talmudicism" on this book. This project was her idea in the first place. To the Seegers and Judith Tick, I am grateful. As with RCS, this edition was not "released" until my wife, Jody Diamond (whose workload seems strangely similar to the above "husband"), edited it thoroughly. I am, once again, deeply appreciative of her help. Though my own daughter, Anna Diamond Polansky, has far fewer than "42 socks and 21 shorts," the part about the bed and the toys rings true. She has helped me in this project more than she knows, singing the songs with me at bedtimes, and in her boundless energy and zest for life, laughingly allowing these folk songs to enter the musical soul of yet another generation.

Ruth Crawford Seeger, later in her "Letter to Miss Prink," remembers that various "operations" with the children are "accompanied by the singing of newly transcribed songs, on their way into the Lomax [in my case, Seeger] book. You wonder if you will do that again when the last sheet of the Appendix [in my case, this edition] is irrevocably out of your grip and you feel like singing again." I am sure she did, and I will too.

Lebanon, New Hampshire
March 9, 2001

Notes

1. Karen Cardullo's "Ruth Crawford Seeger: Preserver of American Folk Music" (Master's Thesis, George Washington University, 1980) includes an excellent, coherent history of American folk song scholarship and transcription as it relates to RCS and this monograph. Cardullo traces many of RCS's stylistic and ideological sources. Judith Tick's biography, *Ruth Crawford Seeger: A Composer's Search for American Music* (New York: Oxford University Press, 1997), is the most extensive, well-written, and deeply researched work to date, not only on this monograph, but on RCS in general. Along with a history of the monograph and its relationship to *OSC*, as well as a careful study of the monograph itself, Tick discusses RCS's influences in the techniques and philosophy of transcription, such as George Herzog, Phillips Barry, Joseph Yasser, Hermann Helmholtz, and Béla Bartók.

2. *American Folk Songs for Children* (1948), *Animal Folk Songs For Children* (1950), *American Folk Songs for Christmas* (1953) (all Garden City, N.Y.: Doubleday).

3. John A. Lomax, "'Sinful Songs' of the Southern Negro," *Musical Quarterly* 20 (April 1934): 177–86. For an interesting discussion of the function of the recording and other aspects of the Lomaxes' early collecting, see Benjamin Filene, "*Our Singing Country*: John and Alan Lomax, Leadbelly, and the Construction of an American Past," *American Quarterly* 43 (December 1991): 602–24.

4. Gene Bluestein, *The Voice of the Folk: Folklore and American Literary Theory* (Amherst: University of Massachusetts Press, 1972), 107.

5. *Ethnomusicology* 43, no. 1 (Winter, 1999): 171–74.

6. Jerrold Hirsch, "Modernity, Nostalgia, and Southern Folklore Studies: The Case of John Lomax," *Journal of American Folklore* 105, no. 415 (Spring, 1992): 183–207.

7. There is even a possibility that RCS worked on the monograph after the publication of *OSC*, perhaps in the hope of independent publication. There is no real evidence at this point for or against this notion. As late as September 30, 1940, in the famous "Letter to Miss Prink," (in the Library of Congress RCS collection, and reprinted in Gaume), RCS refers to it as the "Appendix" ("The Appendix is materially longer . . ."), which, presumably (though not definitely), refers to α.

8. While working on α, RCS probably did not know exactly which of the 300 transcriptions would eventually be included in *OSC*. For example, see her letter to John Becker, September 22, 1939 (reprinted in Gaume, 206):

> My latest musical job has been a fascinating one—that of music editor for the forthcoming-at-MacMillan's book of John and Alan Lomax, "Singing Country" [note neither "This" nor "Our"]. It is a successor to

the "American Ballads and Folksongs" of some years ago, which you may know, and contains about three hundred folk songs which they personally have collected, most of them on discs with their machine in the field, in the country or small town or prison camp. I have transcribed all of them and there are some beauties.

9. Jan Philip Schinhan, ed., "Even the Name Is New: Is It *folk-song* or *folk song* or *folksong*," *The Music of the Ballads,* The Frank C. Brown Collection of North Carolina Folklore, 4 (Durham, N.C.: Duke University Press, 1957), xiii. This famous scholarly collection cites *OSC* and RCS's work extensively in the introduction as an important precedent.

10. Cardullo, in "Ruth Crawford Seeger," quotes from an interview (probably with Charles Seeger, but maybe mistakenly) ascribed to Bess Lomax Hawes, including a succinct summary of the manuscript's history:

The publication was held up until they finally said that if she didn't get this preface done, they would have to publish without it. The preface got longer, and longer, and longer. When she told them about it's [*sic*] length, they said, "Oh heavens, we can't publish more than about three pages." She had already done about 80 pages. It was on the problems of transcriptions.

When she found out they had no intention of publishing more than about three pages, she did the three pages, and the book came out. But the book has certain qualities in the transcriptions she speaks of and studied carefully. (pp. 28–29)

11. See Stephen Wade's excellent notes for Rounder *Treasury.*

12. An awareness of this may have been an impetus for almost fanatical precision and care in transcription. John Lomax pointed out (cited in various sources, including Cardullo): ". . . Mrs. Seeger in some instances played record hundreds of times in an effort to attain perfection in her translation of the tune."

13. Judith Tick, "Ruth Crawford, Charles Seeger, and *The Music of American Folk Songs*," in *Understanding Charles Seeger, Pioneer in American Musicology,* ed. Bell Yung and Helen Rees (Urbana: University of Illinois Press, 1999).

Abbreviations

For detailed information about the sources abbreviated here, see the Editor's Introduction, pp. xxxiv–xxxvii.

α	The earlier, fairly complete typescript entitled "Appendix," located in the Library of Congress.
β	The later, foundational typescript called *The Music of American Folk Song,* in the possession of the Seeger Family.
β-m	Miscellaneous, out of order, probably intermediary pages (between α and β) included at the end of an existing copy of β, in the possession of the Seeger family.
"1001 Folksongs" Papers	Manuscript pages for "1001 Folksongs," an uncompleted project, by RCS with Duncan Emrich and Charles Seeger, still in manuscript. In the possession of the Seeger family.
AFS L[ ]	Library of Congress LP Record Series of songs from the Archive of American Folk Song collection.
Cardullo	Karen Mandeville Cardullo. "Ruth Crawford Seeger: Preserver of American Folk Music." Master's Thesis, George Washington University, 1980.
Charles Seeger's *Check-List*	Charles Seeger's *Check-List of Recorded Songs in the English Language*

	in the Archive of American Folk Song to July, 1940. Washington, D.C.: Music Division, The Library of Congress, 1942.
Gaume	Matilda Gaume. *Ruth Crawford Seeger: Memoirs, Memories, Music.* Metuchen, N.J.: Scarecrow Press, 1986.
Lomax Family Papers	Lomax (John Avery) Family Papers, in the Center for American History, University of Texas at Austin.
"Music Preface" to *Our Singing Country*	Ruth Crawford Seeger. The "Music Preface" published in *Our Singing Country.*
OSC	John and Alan Lomax, eds. *Our Singing Country.* Ruth Crawford Seeger, Music Editor. New York: Macmillan, 1941. Reprint, with a new introduction by Judith Tick. Mineola, N.Y.: Dover, 2000.
RCS	Ruth Crawford Seeger.
Rounder 151[ ]	Compact Disc re-releases of Library of Congress series of songs from the Archive of American Folk Song collection.
Rounder 1821–27	The *Deep River of Song* (The Alan Lomax Collection) anthology on Rounder CDs.
Rounder *Treasury*	*A Treasury of Library of Congress Field Recordings.* Selected and Annotated by Stephen Wade. Rounder 1500 CD.
Tick	Judith Tick. *Ruth Crawford Seeger: A Composer's Search for American Music.* New York: Oxford University Press, 1997.

The Music of American Folk Song

The Music of American Folk Song
by
Ruth Crawford Seeger

Appendix to

Our Singing Country
by
John A. and Alan Lomax
and
Ruth Crawford Seeger

Based on observations made during transcription of three hundred
American folksongs from phonograph recordings in the Archive of
American Folk Song of the Music Division of the Library of Congress

Contents

I. A Note on Transcription[i]

1. The singer and the song

The singers of these songs may be said to have the following characteristics in common:

a. Their singing appears to define a music idiom, or idioms, characteristic at times of geographic region, at times of social stratification.
b. Their individual singing-techniques have, for the most part, been acquired through such processes as the "learning of a song" or the "composing of a song," or the singing and re-singing of songs already learned or "composed." While there is abundant evidence of application in the practice and study of the idiom, this study appears not to be consciously regarded as such by the possessors of the idiom.
c. Their repertoire, in a vast majority of cases, has been acquired by means of no other written technique than that of language—and, in many cases, with no written technique at all. The "learning of a song" has been, thus, in the main "by ear," and in conformity with prevailing oral traditions. It is reasonably certain that few could read or write any music notation, or that they learned the songs from singers who could read or write it.

Passed on year after year from one person to another, a majority of the songs can be said to have been modified in many ways, and to styles of performance in the singing any one song can differ radically, with the result that the lineage of the song is[ii] at times hard to detect. Occasional performances can, in fact, become so highly individual that the question will arise whether the singer may be said to have "composed" a new song. It would be of interest to trace the identity of some one tune as "common possession" through a series of such variations in style of performance, and to attempt to determine whether and at what point it may be felt to have taken on a sufficiently different character to allow classification as a "new" tune, and, therefore,[iii] claim of composition by its singer. It would appear that many claims of this sort would be found to constitute a normal step in some such process. Invention, composition indeed, there certainly has been, but mainly as added increment to a current stock or repertoire unaffected, except in rare instances, by considerations of authorship, copyright, publication or critical review.

2. Phonographic recording of the song

With thirteen exceptions,[1] the songs in this edition were recorded by John A. and Alan Lomax, and the original recordings have been deposited in the Archive of American Folk Song in the Music Division of The Library of Congress. Copies of these, as of many other recordings in the Archive, are available to students.

With the same thirteen exceptions, the songs were transcribed from duplicate discs of these original recordings.[v]

3. Transcription of the song from phonographic recording

a. Transcription from phonograph recording versus dictation direct from folk singer, player or intermediary

It is becoming increasingly recognized[2] that transcription from phonograph recording, as compared with dictation direct from folk singer or intermediary, is capable of giving a more accurate and objective picture of the song *and of its style of performance*. Transcription from recording affords a notation of one singing of a song as sung by one singer or group of singers. Dictation from the folk singer

---

1. These are: included from other publications: *Down, Down, Down*; *The High Barbaree*; *Over Jordan*; *The Romish Lady*; dictated to the transcriber by the singer: *Bugger Burns*; *Cotton Eyed Joe*; *Godamighty Drag*; *I Got to Roll*; *Old Bangham*; *Old King Cole*; *Po' Farmer*;[iv] transcribed from commercial recordings: *The Sporting Cowboy* and *Hard Times in the Country*.

2. See, for instance, George Herzog, "Research in Primitive and Folk Music in the United States," *American Council of Learned Societies Bulletin* No. 24 (1936): 45ff.[vi]

or intermediary affords, in most cases, a composite of several singings of a song by one singer or group of singers, or sometimes of the collector's memory of such. The transcription (notation) made from the recording can be checked and re-checked by the transcriber for accuracy and for the finer nuances which are vital attributes of the singing-style, and which on first hearing may well elude him, especially when dealing with the more complex singing-styles. In dictation, checking or re-checking is problematical. Transcription from the recording offers, in addition, the possibility of check by others upon the work of the transcriber. Dictation from the singer is scarcely ever subject to such check.

b. Transcription through graph notation[vii]

The most accurate techniques of transcription from phonograph recording are, of course, the modern graphing techniques, now perfected for laboratory use but not generally available.

These show a thing which musicians have always vaguely felt to be true—namely, that a tune is a stream of sound whose variations in pitch and in time can be represented on paper as a curving line. If these techniques had been used in preparation of this collection of transcriptions, the first draft of a tune would appear as in Figure 1.[3,viii]

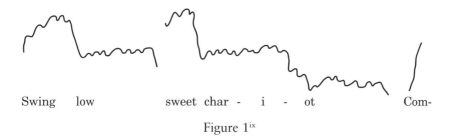

Swing   low   sweet char - i - ot   Com-

Figure 1[ix]

Reduction to customary music notation would have involved, first, the levelling off of the smaller curves on the lines which indicate the vibrato of the voice.

---

3. After Milton Metfessel, *Phonophotography in Folk Music* (Chapel Hill: University of North Carolina Press, 1928), 62.

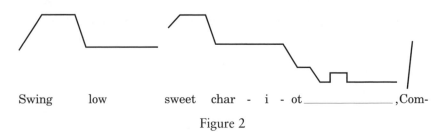

Swing   low   sweet   char - i - ot_____ ,Com-

Figure 2

This would give a series of plateaus upon which we could pick out points to be represented by notes.

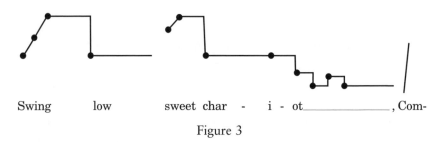

Swing   low   sweet char   -   i - ot_____ , Com-

Figure 3

At this point, the musician could join in the work with the laboratory specialist. He is used to working with diagrams such as the above, though not with such accurate ones. Many of the more subtle variations of pitch and time would have to be disregarded before the relative durations of these notes could be fixed, and the bar-lines be placed upon a conventional music staff.

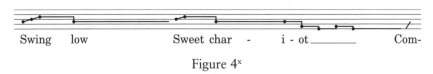

Swing   low   Sweet char   -   i - ot_____   Com-

Figure 4[x]

The points can at this stage be replaced by notes, and the lines by note values.

Swing   low sweet   char - i - ot_____   Com-

Figure 5[xi]

Figure 5 represents, within a margin of error of approximately .1 second, metrical irregularities observed in the original singing. The notation is still too complex for a reading public, which demands some simplification as that shown in Figure 6.

Figure 6

4. The reader and the song

From the above analysis it must be apparent what a small part of the original song and its manner of singing is represented to the reader in customary notation, especially when dealing with the freer singing-styles. In the most elaborate of these, notation with a view to readability and singability often strips the song of many or most of the finer subtleties of its particular style of performance, and leaves not much more than a skeleton of the original singing. Even songs in the less complex styles lose, in such notation, many or all of the characteristics, rhythmic and tonal, of their manner of singing. Thus, the frequently heard extended tone (i.e., a tone whose extension introduces a temporary irregularity of meter within the framework of an established regular meter) is clipped of its "extra" time-value; the simple slide (accented initial and accented final) is written as a single tone;[xii] or the "blue note," and the neutral tone, is tailored to fit our twelve-tone system of notation—and, if possible, to fit a seven-tone scale within that system. Whether, and to what extent, such "trimming down" of tunes in notation can account for opinions expressed from time to time as to "lack of subtlety" in the music itself, is a question not yet answered—as also, the extent to which such judgments are based upon acquaintance with printed collections rather than with the singing itself.

Some simplification is, of course, inevitable. Decision as to how much involves a number of considerations. It is often far from clear, for instance, in the analysis of any particular case, just where "the song" can be said to end and its singing to begin. It is further a question, not only how many characteristics of singing-style can be indicated without cluttering the notations, but also how many of those should be indicated and how many left to be filled in on the basis of the reader's knowledge (or lack of knowledge!) of the idiom. Certainly, re-creation of the tune by the reader must depend to no small extent on his ability to put back upon the more or less skeleton notation such "flesh, blood and nerve fibre" as can best approximate for him the character of the original song and its singing. His ability to do this will be in direct ratio to the degree to which he is, or may become, familiar with the idiomatic variations of American folk singing.[xiii]

He will, in all probability, be a city or town dweller. He will be used to reading books, and may be able to read music notation more or less well. He may be thoroughly familiar with—may, in fact, even be a student of—one or more of the idioms employed. Or he may scarcely be conscious of their existence. In either case, when he sings these songs there will be a tendency to fill in the notations with unconscious approximations of fine-art singing—partly because well-educated Americans have been taught that only fine-art music is "music" or "good music," and partly because he is accustomed to associating music notation only with the mannerisms of fine-art music.

In the tempering of this tendency, the reader may turn for aid as well as enjoyment to the many phonograph recordings of American folk music now available.[4,xiv] Upon first hearing many of them, he will no doubt be inclined, because of his greater acquaintance with fine-art music, either to overlook (as of little value) or to smile at (as quaint) or to look down upon (as "common," not "refined") or even to scorn (as "out-of-tune"—i.e., with accepted fine-art tunings) many of the mannerisms and subtleties of this singing. He will, in addition, note the absence of many mannerisms common to fine-art performance. He will, for instance, find that most of the singers on these recordings sing without "expression"—i.e., expression in the manner of fine-art singing. He will miss the continual fluctuation of mood so prevalent in fine-art performance, the frequent formalized slowing-down for "effect" at ends of phrases and stanzas, the drama of constant change from soft to loud and back again, the rounded bel canto tone-quality of the "well-trained" voice. Upon repeated hearing, however, it is possible that such omissions may come to take on for him positive rather than negative value. He may begin to see in them signs of strength rather than of weakness. He may even discover that he likes this music for these very omissions—and may find himself singing along with it. Whether, finally, he comes to

---

4. An extensive list of commercial recordings, compiled by Alan Lomax, can be obtained from the Archive of American Folk Song in the Music Division of The Library of Congress. As stated previously, copies of many recordings in the Archive are also available.

define much of it in terms of epic quality is not of such import, in the present discussion, as is the probability that, through this closer acquaintance with American folk singing, his re-creation from notation of similar songs in similar idioms will undoubtedly ring truer and "come more natural" than before.

5. Music notation as a bridge

Music notations of folk songs serve, then, as a bridge between, mainly, two different types of singers. Over this bridge a vital heritage of culture can pass, from the rural people who, for the most part, have preserved it, to the urban people who have more or less lost it and wish to recapture it.

A great deal depends upon just how this bridge is built. It must compensate not only for the gap between the types of singers, but also for as many as possible of the technical shortcomings of the system of notation itself, which, as has been shown above, are especially apparent when we try to use it in connection with an idiom with which it has not customarily been associated.

The manner of its building must be determined, for the most part, by the specific use to which the notations will be put. If they are to be used for strictly scientific study rather than for singing, the transcriber will wish to include in them all details—rhythmic, tonal and formal—perceptible to him. If they are to be published in song books for school or community use, he will no doubt feel constrained to indicate only the outline, the bare skeleton of the song. It has been the aim, in transcribing this collection of songs, to follow a course *midway between these extremes: to catch a just balance which will convey as much as possible of the rich complexity of the folk singer's art, yet in simple enough terms to allow ready grasp by the interested amateur.* The selection of points, or notes, along the various curves of the tunes in this collection of transcriptions represents, therefore, one particular transcriber's judgment as to the best way to build a bridge in accordance with this aim—a bridge which will enable the average person, unfamiliar with the tune or with the idiom, to make his closest possible approximation of the original singing.

It is obvious that such a bridge must be neither too complex nor too simple. It involves the making of notations *which are comparatively easy to read at sight, yet which include some of the simpler characteristics of singing-style as revealed in the recordings from which the tunes are transcribed.* The scholar, as noted above, would call for more points along the line. This, however, would in many cases prevent the notations serving the aim stated above. It has often been remarked that too much small detail discourages the average reader of music notation. He loses the concept of the whole— the flow. In the words of the old adage, he cannot see the forest for the trees.

On the other hand, too great simplification in notation results in his not even seeing the trees, for the piles of logs they have been sawed into.[xv]

6. Three basic types of transcription illustrated

Transcription of a single song with a view to three such widely varying objectives as those set forth above, gives interesting results, especially among the more complex singing-styles. In each of the following illustrations, transcription A is decidedly difficult to read, and transcription C is highly simplified. Transcription B represents a point more or less midway between these extremes.[xvi]

The Negro work song *Pauline* is perhaps the best example of ornate vocal technique to be found among these recordings.[xvii]

[Figure 7 {*Pauline*}, not extant]

The Negro holler *Make Me a Garment*[xviii] shows somewhat less ornate vocal technique, but greater metrical irregularity. Alternatives of B and C are given.

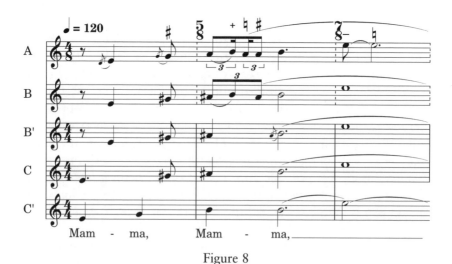

Figure 8

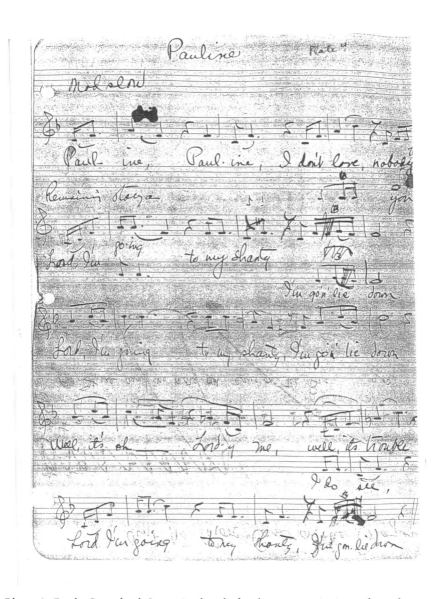

Plate 4. Ruth Crawford Seeger's sketch for her transcription of *Pauline* (actual transcription, Figure 7, not extant). (Photo, Lomax [John Avery] Family Papers, Center for American History, University of Texas at Austin. Used by permission.)

Figure 8 *(continued)*

Somewhat less ornate in both respects is the Negro holler *Trouble, Trouble.*

Figure 9

The Cajun song *Belle*[xix] exhibits a metrical irregularity less elastic than that of the above two songs, but exceptional among these recordings for the consistency with which the singer adheres to it from stanza to stanza throughout the recording. The singing-style may be said to be about midway between the complex and the simple.

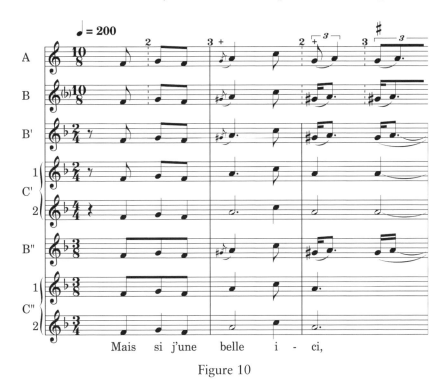

Figure 10

Belle, c'est par rap - port à toi, Belle,

Figure 10 *(continued)*

Plate 5. Page 14 from α, showing Ruth Crawford Seeger's handwritten transcription of *Belle*, Figure 10. (Photo, Seeger family. Used by permission.)

Although of an entirely different character, *Three Nights Drunk* and *Long Lonesome Road* may also be felt to represent styles of performance about midway between the complex and the simple. Throughout these songs there is about as much singing off-the-beat as on it. Transcriptions of three degrees of accuracy are given.

Sad - dle on a ⏜ milk cow's back I nev-er did see be - fore.

Figure 11

Hang down your head and cry, my Lord,

Figure 12

The singing of the white spiritual *O Lovely Appearance of Death* and of the ballad *John Riley* also provide interesting examples.[xx]

Figure 13

Figure 14[xxi]

Similar transcriptions of songs in simpler singing-styles provide illustration none-the-less valuable for the narrower limits of variation involved. The first of the following examples is from *Dark-Eyed Canaller*.[xxii] The second is from *Adieu to the Stone Walls*, whose style of performance is more or less typical of the simplest manners of singing heard on these recordings.

Figure 15

Figure 16

7. Song-norm

Illustrations such as these bring up inevitably the subject of what we might call song-norm, or basic tune-pattern. Styles of performance in the singing of any one song can differ as widely as do transcription-types A, B or C in any of the above examples. Furthermore, as is well known, further study of the tunes of most songs, with respect to basic or commonly possessed tune-pattern, can usually reveal the existence of other songs under other titles with other texts, whose tune-patterns show varying degrees of similarity to that of the tune under discussion.[5] *Pauline* is an example of such a song. There are recordings of songs under the title *Pauline* and under other titles with other texts, whose tune-patterns resemble that of Prothero's[xxiv] *Pauline* sufficiently to allow their classification with it in one group or tune-family. In comparison with these recordings, Prothero's singing of the song (see transcription A, Figure 7)[xxv] would appear to be an involved embroidering of a more or less simple and, apparently, commonly possessed tune-pattern.

This question of "common possession" versus "individual contribution" must, obviously, be a consideration in an inquiry as to where may be said to lie the song-norm within any one family of tunes. Such inquiry must involve, first, determination of the norm within each separate song in the tune-family, as sung by each of the various singers. This must, in turn, involve determination of the norm within each separate musical function (rhythmic, tonal, formal).[6] A strong deciding factor in such a study is that of *majority usage,* especially with respect to interstanzaic variation.

8. Majority usage[xxvii]

As is well known, a folk singer is seldom found to sing all stanzas of any one song in precisely the same manner. Even among the simpler singing-styles, in which the tune-pattern remains more or less the same from stanza to stanza, a certain amount of interstanzaic variation is heard within one or more of the musical functions.[7] In some songs, one such variation, occurring within the same musical function and at the same point in the tune of each stanza, may be found to be different at each recurrence.[xxviii] In other songs, the variation (occurring within the same musical function and at the same point in the tune) will be found to agree in two stanzas or more. When the variation thus agrees in a preponderant number of stanzas, *majority usage* may be felt to point to that variation as being representative, within that musical function and at that point in the tune, of the song in its entirety (i.e., as sung through from the first to the last stanza).

Thus, when an entire song must be represented by the tune of only one of its stanzas, this factor of majority usage can be seen to

---

5. See for instance George Pullen Jackson, *White Spirituals in the Southern Up-lands* (Chapel Hill: University of North Carolina Press, 1953), 246–73.[xxiii]

6. See Sections [10–12].[xxvi]

7. See Section 25.

bear weight, not only upon such simple interstanzaic-variational questions as that shown in measure 16 of *As I Went Out for a Ramble*,[xxix]

Figure 17

but upon further problems of interstanzaic variation as are presented by the following instances:

a. a major tendency in the singing of some stanzas, as against a minor in the singing of others (as heard in the recordings of *Go Down, Ol' Hannah, Blanche Comme la Neige, The Bachelor's Lay* and many other songs as sung by both Negro and white singers);

b. a more complex metrical pattern in the singing of several stanzas, as against a simpler pattern in another (as on the recording of *Fare Ye Well, My Darlin'*);

c. occasional deviation from an established meter in the singing of some stanzas, as against continued adherence to it in others (as on the recording of *Sweet William*);

d. rhythmic interstanzaic variation in relative tone-durations within the limits of the measure-length—involving no deviation from an established meter (as in well over half the songs in this collection);

e. interstanzaic variation in rest duration—involving no deviation from an established meter (as in measure 4 of *My Father Gave Me a Lump of Gold*);

f. interstanzaic variation in location and length of extended tone and of extended or inserted rest—involving deviation from an established meter (as in *The Irish Lady*);

g. interstanzaic variation in location and type of slides and ornaments (as in *Diamond Joe* and many other songs).

As can be seen, this list could be extended. All aspects in the singing of the song can be seen[xxx] to be concerned with this factor, in the selection of the model tune.

9. Underlimits of amount of detail shown in notation, especially with regard to the simpler singing-styles

Such songs as Prothero's *Pauline* are representative, with respect to complexity, of less than one-tenth of the songs in this collection. The remainder are in more or less simple singing-styles. Within this majority group of simpler songs, such elimination of detail as has been felt necessary in realization of the aim stated in Section 6, has consisted mainly in omission of:

a. deviations of less than a half-step from the tunings accepted for use in occidental fine-art music;[xxxi]
b. deviations of less than a beat from an established measure-length, in moderately fast or fast tempo;
c. certain extended tones and extended or inserted rest[s], when appearing so irregularly or so rarely from stanza to stanza that their inclusion in the notation of any one stanza would be misleading;
d. certain complex types of anticipation and delaying of beat;
e. complex waverings in the voice, and many unaccented slides to and from the clearly established, and therefore notated, tones of the tune.[8]

Within the minority group of more complex songs,[xxxii] greater subtlety of detail has occasionally been allowed in notation. Inclusion of a few transcriptions of this sort has been felt to be essential, not only as examples of the manners in which songs of similar type may be sung, but also with a view to dispelling the occasionally expressed belief in the "simplicity" of American folk singing, and to

---

8. More detailed discussion of each of these points may be found in Sections 28, 21c, 23, 19, and 27 respectively.

give an idea of some types of technical integration (tonal, rhythmic, formal) which further study can reveal to the student. The greater number of these songs are Negro hollers (as *Make Me a Garment,* or *Trouble, Trouble*). There are also a few blues (as *I Been a Bad, Bad Girl*). The work song *Pauline* is closely allied to the holler through its style of performance.

10. The model tune as representative of the song as a whole

Scientific study requires transcription of the music of all stanzas— of all singers, if more than one, and of the complete accompaniment, if any. The school or community song book, on the other hand, has room for and needs one tune only, which may or may not be a modification of the tune of one or of several stanzas, or a composite of several, depending on the taste of its editor and the requirements of its use.

Here again, in this collection of transcriptions, attempt was made to establish a type of choice midway between the extremes. Most of the songs are represented by a transcription of a *model tune*—i.e., *by the tune of one single stanza of one song as sung in one performance.*[9]

---

9. See Section 12 for exceptions in the form of composite tunes. In addition, ten songs have been given transcription of the tunes of two stanzas (as *Mamma, Mamma,* and *Make Me a Garment*), one, of the tune of three stanzas (*The Rising Sun Blues*). Several songs, such as *Job* and *Dig My Grave,*[xxxiii] have been given more comprehensive transcription. Two recordings have been transcribed in full from beginning to end (*John Done Saw That Number* and *Trouble, Trouble*), including the chanting in the former and the mule shout of the latter. Insterstanzaic variations have been appended only when felt to be indispensable to the singing of later stanzas (as in *Black Jack Davy* and *Tee Roo*).

Of the twenty-one songs sung by two or more voices, "in parts," twelve have been given transcription of all principal (continuous) parts heard on the recording. Of these twelve songs transcribed in parts, five were sung by two singers (*Adam in the Garden Pinnin' Leaves; Holy Ghost; Johnnie, Won't You Ramble; Round the Bay of Mexico; Texas Rangers*); one was sung by three singers (*Dig My Grave*); the remainder were sung by larger groups (*Biddy, Biddy, Don't Talk About It; God Moves on the Water; Ladies in the Dinin' Room; Married Man Gonna Keep Your Secret; The Wind Blow East*). The nine part-songs not transcribed in parts: (*Big Fat Woman; Dem Bones; Didn' Ol' John Cross the Water on his Knees?; God Don't Like It; John Was a-Writin'; Little Bonny; Look Down That Lonesome Road; O Lawd I Went Up on the Mountain; Take This Hammer*).

The term "in parts" is here used to signify continuous or consistent deviation from unison or octave singing, and possesses no harmony-book implications. Choice of model stanza in part-songs was based upon considerations of all elements in the polyphonic fabric (as in *Married Man Gonna Keep Your Secret,* whose hummed obligato is best heard toward the middle of the recording). No composites, either

11. The initial tune as model tune

Decision as to whether the model tune shall also be the *initial tune* (i.e., the tune of the first stanza)[xxxiv] involves a number of considerations. Certainly, it is desirable that the tune and the text which are sung together on the recording should also appear together in the notation. Yet, not infrequently, considerations of majority usage point to the tune of some later stanza as being more representative of the song as a whole. Other factors—as, for instance, requirements of readability or singability (as in *Roustabout Holler*) or "error,"[10] incompleteness or lack of clarity in singing or recording of the initial tune (as in *Tom Bolyn* or *Haul Away, My Rosy*)—also advise at times the use of some other than the initial tune.

In twenty-three songs in this collection, the tune selected as model tune is not the initial tune heard on the recording. Rhythmic likenesses between words of the initial and of the later tune, as well as ease in accommodating to the latter the remainder of the text, have been determining factors in this selection of a model tune from among later stanzas.[11] Strongest determining factor has, here again, been that of majority usage.

---

horizontal or vertical, were allowed in transcription of part-songs, since a change in one part concerns all other parts.

10. In a few songs, all stanzas excepting stanza 1 are sung to the same tune-pattern, the initial tune appearing only once on the recording.

At times it would appear that the singer of such a song simply "got off to a bad start" on the wrong tune, correcting his mistake at the second stanza—as in *I Came to This Country in 1865*, whose first phrase-ending (and no other) is strongly reminiscent of *The Buffalo Skinners*. It is a question whether this is also the case with *The Wild Colonial Boy*; *Georgia Land*;[xxxv] and *Run Along, You Little Dogies* (whose differing portions are more extensive than those in the above song, and have been included in their notations).

At other times—as in *The Vance Song* and *Johnny Stiles*—it would appear, rather, that the singer, after his first complete statement of a full four-phrase tune, has returned to the middle of the tune instead of the beginning and has "got stuck" on these last two phrases from then on to the end of the song, repeating them over and over to the exclusion of the first two. (The full four-phrase tune has been notated in each of those songs).

11. These points have been of value in selection of model tunes for the songs *Doney Gal*; *The Crooked Gun*; *Dupree*; *Duncan and Brady*; *The Beaver Island Boys*; *Ain't It Hard to be a Right Black Nigger?*; and *Diamond Joe* in which the compiling of texts from several sources has required placement beneath the music of words which do not appear on the recording used for transcription of the music.

12. The composite tune

The making of composite tunes has been avoided in transcription of the songs in this collection. A few exceptions[12] have been allowed, due mainly to considerations of majority usage and of readability or singability. In these exceptions, a small section from the tune of one stanza has been replaced by a parallel section from the tune of one other stanza. Sections from more than two stanzas have not been composited. In all but two songs, such sections comprise less than two measures.[13] As stated previously, no compositing has been allowed in transcription of part-songs.

13. The transcriber and a changing oral tradition

That the single stanza must appear as representative of an entire song, is occasionally deplored—not the least by the transcriber, to whom the concept of a song not infrequently comes to include all stanzas as essential parts of a whole. The "freezing" of the song into the mold of one of these stanzas, and subsequent presentation of this to the reader as "the song," is a task he is at times reluctant to perform.

It is a question, however, whether this practice is so foreign to the spirit of oral tradition as might seem to be the case. For, while it may be supposed that some folk singers learn their tunes complete with all their variations, others certainly learn a single tune and fit all stanzas to it, while still others learn a single tune and proceed to make their own variations, sometimes varying these variations at each performance. That the reader be expected to compensate for elimination (through use of a model or composite tune) of these interstanzaic variations, would, in a specious way, appear to be in accordance, then, with processes current in oral tradition.

The variations introduced by the reader will, undoubtedly, not always be in keeping with oral tradition. It is the nature of oral tra-

---

12. These are: (1) *Soon One Morning, Death Come Creepin'*; (2) *Choose You a Seat 'n' Set Down*; (3) *Don't Talk About It*; (4) *Long Summer Day*;[xxxvi] (5) *The Rich Old Lady*; (6) *I'm Worried Now, But I Won't Be Worried Long*; (7) *Katy Dorey*; (8) *The Vance Song*; (9) *Job*; (10) *The Coal Miner's Child*; (11) *Sweet William*.

13. In the first song in Footnote 12, the section composited comprises one 8th note and one 16th; in (2), a quarter note; in (3) and (4), a half measure; in (5), a half measure and an 8th note; in (6) and (7), two-thirds of a measure; in (8), one measure; in (9), one measure and a quarter; in (10), three measures; in (11), four measures.

dition, however, to change. It seems hard to deny that this change can be said to involve, and to have been involved in, a two-way process. Certainly, some songs have come "down" (and will continue to do so) from popular and fine-art idioms, and have been made "common" through processes of oral tradition. The mere fact that we have not a written record of the reverse process should not, of itself, allow us to jump to the conclusion that "common" songs have not also found their way "up" (and will continue to do so) from folk into popular and fine-art idioms. Many observations over a considerable period of time incline the present writer to give equal emphasis to both trends. More and more city people are learning folk songs. And more and more country people are learning the ways of popular and fine-art music, composed, in many cases, by the city people who have learned the folk music, or who came originally from the country, bringing with them, consciously or unconsciously, a degree of familiarity with folk music.

In the operation of these trends, judgements will vary as to which characteristics of the various idioms are being lost, which modified and which preserved. Each individual will have his own preferences in respect to what should be lost, modified or preserved. A transcriber is no exception, and consciously or unconsciously expresses his own preferences, supporting one or the other of these trends, thus influencing, in his small way, their operation. A person of antiquarian tastes will tend to emphasize the archaic and to discard the new. The fine-art composer will tend to emphasize the unusual, the new, and to discard the "ordinary."[xxxvii] The comparative musicologist will try to present as objectively as possible all the data exhibited by each individual performance, and to subordinate his own taste reactions. The connoisseur of the repertoire, on the other hand, may feel that his own taste reaction is of the highest importance, and may wish to present the song, not as an individual performance by an individual singer, but as a generic thing of which he, the connoisseur, has formed a conception as an almost independent entity floating through the time and space of the American scene.

In decisions upon details of transcription of this collection of songs, recognition has been given to the above interests, with a view to uniformity of treatment. Evaluation of these interests, as also of the aim set forth in Section 6 as basis for work on this particular collection of transcriptions, must take into consideration the widespread influence of the radio on styles of performance. For the radio is giving more and more attention to the materials of American folk music. It seems, in fact, that an American folk music "boom" is at hand.[xxxviii] But it will be noted (especially on programs on the larger stations) that fine-art standards of performance are, for the most part, either set up or encouraged. Rough edges are not tolerated. The song must be polite, "slick," proper—not only from a textual but from a musical standpoint. It would appear, therefore, that, while recognizing that both oral and written traditions will and must change, the writing down of oral tradition should be of such a character that it may foster rather than work against that tradition.[xxxix]

II. Notes on the Songs and on Manners of Singing

14. Adherence to a dynamic level throughout the song as a whole

With few exceptions, the singers of these songs maintain approximately the same level of loudness or softness from phrase to phrase and from stanza to stanza throughout the song. The calculated gradations of broad dynamic levels so characteristic of fine-art performance, with emphasis on climax and morendo, is not typical of the folk singing recorded on these discs.[xl]

Among the freer singing-styles will be found recordings which exhibit considerable dynamic detail *within the phrase*—as, for instance, that of *Darling Corey,* a fragment of which is given below, with dynamics roughly indicated,

Figure 18

and of the exceptional *Go Down, You Little Red Rising Sun*:

Figure 19

The dynamic change in stanza 4 of *Go Down, Ol' Hannah,* though slightly more extensive, is still within the limits of the phrase.

Figure 20

II

NOTES ON THE SONGS AND ON MANNERS OF SINGING

14. <u>Adherence to a dynamic level throughout the song as a whole</u>

With few exceptions, the singers of these songs maintain approximately the same level of loudness or softness from phrase to phrase and from stanza to stanza throughout the song. The calculated gradations of broad dynamic levels so characteristic of fine-art performance, with emphasis on climax and morendo, is not typical of the folk singing recorded on these discs.

Among the freer singing-styles will be found recordings which exhibit considerable dynamic detail <u>within the phrase</u> – as, for instance, that of <u>Darling Corey</u>, a fragment of which is given below, with dynamics roughly indicated,

Figure 18

and of the exceptional <u>Go Down, You Little Red Rising Sun</u>:

Figure 19

Plate 6. Beginning of second section "Notes on Songs and the Manners of Singing," from α. (Photo, Seeger family. Used by permission.)

15. Adherence to a dramatic level throughout the song as a whole

With few exceptions, the singer sets the dramatic mood at the beginning of the song and maintains that mood throughout. Dramatization in the conventional style of fine-art performance, with emphasis on fluctuation of mood, is scarcely ever heard on these discs.

The singer does not try to make the song mean more, or less, than it does. No special emphasis is given to words or to details which the sophisticated singer would tend to point up. The strong dramatic conviction with which the singer begins his song underlies each stanza from first to last; the gay stanza, or the comic, is sung in precisely the same manner of musical expression as the tragic or dignified. The tune makes no compromises, is no slower nor faster, no softer nor louder. There is no climax—the song "just stops."[xli]

The few exceptions to this general practice which do occur will be found, for the most part, among the come-all-ye's and the Negro hollers. Experience with this collection would suggest, however, that even among these freer songs, fluctuation of mood is more often induced by musical than by linguistic requirements.[14]

16. Adherence to the tempo set at the beginning of the song

a. Infrequency of long ritardandos from the beginning to the end of the song as a whole

The singer, once he has set his tempo, usually sticks to it throughout the song without substantial deviation. Metronomic testing of the first and last stanzas of each of these recordings has shown that, aside from the few tunes in which no regular pulse or beat can be said to have been established (see Section 17), the collection contains few exceptions to this statement. And it will be noted in these exceptions, that the singer increases rather than decreases his speed (see the recording of *Dig My Grave*).[xlii] Such tempo changes have been indicated immediately following the metronome marks at the heading of the song.

b. Infrequency of short stereotyped ritardandos at ends of phrases and stanzas

The practice of making short, frequent, stereotyped ritardandos at ends of phrases and stanzas—a convention so common among sophisticated singers—is rarely found in these recordings. *Peter Gray,* in which a formal ritardando recurs at the end of each stanza, was sung by a college professor. *Texas Rangers,* which contains a formal ritardando at the end of the last stanza, was sung by two young girls

---

14. See also Phillips Barry, "American Folk Music," *Southern Folklore Quarterly* 1, no. 2 (1937): 42–43.

whose style of performance suggests radio influence, although they are not themselves radio performers. *Ladies in the Dinin' Room* shows a less formal ritardando at the end of the last stanza. The light ritardando at the end of each stanza of *Old Shoes and Leggin's* has been written into the metrical frame (see Figure 21(a)): it appears to be effected for the most part by extension of tone. In Figure 21(b), is shown what might be felt to be the underlying metrical pattern, with ritardando less precisely indicated. The ritardando in *Peter Gray* has been notated in the latter fashion.

Figures 21(a) and 21(b)[xliii]

17. Strict time and free singing styles

Unless otherwise indicated at the heading of the notation, the singer should be understood to have sung the song more or less "in strict time, well accented" (tempo giusto).

The twenty-nine songs departing from this practice—i.e., in which the tempo is either (a) vague or indeterminate, or (b) established, departed from and returned to periodically throughout the stanza (rubato)—have been marked "Free" and "Somewhat free." These songs are about evenly distributed among Negro and white, the majority of the former being hollers, and about half of the latter partaking to greater or lesser degree of characteristics of rubato-parlando singing-style, of which the singer of the come-all-ye[15] makes

---

15. See Phillips Barry, "American Folk Music."

especially insistent use. Among the remaining half by white singers are such songs as *Katy Dorey, Pay Day at Coal Creek,*[xliv] and *Old Shoes and Leggin's.* It is to be noted that both the come-all-ye's and the holler belong to unaccompanied tradition, which may to some extent account for their rhythmic freedom.

It might be of interest to trace, through study of the recordings of several representative songs either bordering upon or belonging to one of these groups, the nature and scope of the varying degrees of rhythmic freedom or fluidity found within the group. Take, for instance, the five songs *The Wild Colonial Boy, Hog Rogues on the Harricane, The Crooked Gun,*[xlv] *The Little Brown Bulls* and *The "Bigler,"*[16,xlvi] of which the last-named is an excellent example of rubato-parlando singing-style.

The first of these, *The Wild Colonial Boy,* shows in its singing a negligible amount of rhythmic freedom. The extended tones (see Section 23[xlvii]) appear to be superimposed upon an otherwise straightforward metrical fabric, the duration of beat and of subdivision of beat remaining comparatively constant. The first stanza of the second song, *Hog Rogues on the Harricane,* exhibits in its singing a slightly greater rhythmic elasticity within the measure; the duration of the measure remains, however, fairly constant. As the song proceeds, elasticity increases, affecting the measure—sometimes shortening, sometimes lengthening its duration. The singing of the third song, *The Crooked Gun,* partakes unmistakably of rubato-parlando style of performance. Here, sections of one-and-a-half to two measures are periodically hastened, with greater freedom within their various parts than that shown in *Hog Rogues on the Harricane.* The extended tone, most often interposed between such two-measure sections, begins to take on the compensatory character indicative of true rubato; the general effect is one of a moderate amount of rhythmic fluidity. In the singing of the fourth song, *The Little Brown Bulls,* rhythmic freedom consists rather in the variation in length and in location of the extended tones, the intervening passages remaining more or less stable rhythmically. (The metronome, if set at the quarter-note unit, is found to be fairly consistently adhered to from beginning to end.) The rubato hastenings and haltings found in *The Crooked Gun* are not typical of this song; yet one may conjecture to

---

16. Notations of these songs will be found at the end of this volume, beginning at page [ ]. It should be remembered, however, that the above discussion is based *upon the recording* and *upon consideration of the songs as a whole,* of which the notation is, obviously, but a small part.

what extent the varying lengths and placement of the extended tones take on among themselves compensatory values (see Section 21). The effect of the song as a whole is one of greater rhythmic freedom that that given by *The Crooked Gun*—though, it might be said, not of such fluidity. Finally, in the singing of the fifth song, *The "Bigler,"* rhythmic fluidity and freedom are so inherent a feature that indication of beat, or subdivision of beat or of measure must be taken more as a learning aid than as a suggestion of an underlying pattern which the singer can be conceived of as departing from or adhering to. Here is constant give and take, and an excellent example of rubato-parlando singing-style.

18. Pulse and count

The basis for determination of measure and of count in these transcriptions has been the pulse—or foot-beat, sometimes clearly heard in the tapping of the foot, as on the recording of *If I Got My Ticket, Can I Ride?*

Figure 22[xlviii]

but more often implied by the usually strong metrical accents in the singing itself, as in *Lolly Too-Dum*[xlix] and many other songs.

Figure 23

In each of the notations, the note-value employed as unit of measurement of metronomic speed, and so indicated at the heading of each song (as ♩ = 66 or ♩ = 108[l])[17] should be understood to represent the predominant pulse felt in the singing of that song. In most of the notations, the note-value indicated by the denominator of the metrical signature will be found to be the same as that employed in indication of the metronomic speed—and, therefore, also to represent the pulse (as in (b) and (d) of Figure 24). When the denominator of the metrical signature does not thus correspond with the unit of measurement of the metronomic speed, the latter will be the reader's guide as to pulse. A considerable number of such exceptions have been allowed (see (a) and (c) of Figure 24, also Figures 22, 23 and many others), since such unaccustomed meters as 1/2 and 1/3 have been felt to be out of place in these notations. (See further, Section 20, Footnote 27.)[li]

Determination of the length of beams connecting the 8th, 16th and 32nd notes has, with few exceptions, been upon the basis of pulse. Thus:

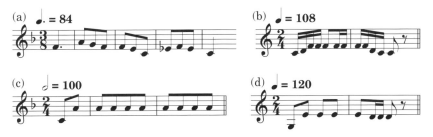

Figure 24[18]

To enable the reader to obtain at first glance a general idea of the relative speed of each song, it has been felt important to base the

17. The eleven songs not transcribed from phonograph recordings have not been given metronome indications. These are listed in Footnote 1 of Section 1.

18. Songs illustrated in Figure 24 are as follows: (a) *The Bachelor's Lay*; (b) *Daddy Shot a Bear*; (c) *Don't You Like It*; (d) *Hush Li'l Baby*.

choice of note-value employed as metrical unit of measurement (i.e., as to whether a song in triple time be written as 3/2, 3/4 or 3/8, or a song in duple time be written in 2/2, 2/4 or 2/8, etc.) upon some consistent practice followed throughout the collection of transcriptions as a whole. With a few exceptions,[19] a pulse or foot-beat of less than M.M. 100 has been represented by the half-note (as $\downarrow$ = 80); a pulse of more than M.M. 100, by the quarter-note (as $\downarrow$ = 108).[lii]

19. Anticipation and delay of beat

In most of the songs sung by Negro singers, and in a large number of those sung by white singers, there is more singing off the beat than on the beat, the regular pulse remaining, however, fairly steady. In their more complex forms, or when occurring so frequently throughout a song that the page would be confusingly cluttered with minute rhythmic complexities, these anticipations and delayings of beat have been considered as general characteristics of singing-style, and not suitable to notation of the type used in transcription of most of these songs. In their simpler forms they have—more or less sparingly—been incorporated in the notations, as guides to singing-style. A few examples of these are given below; (a), (b), (d), (e), (i) and (h) taken from notations of songs by Negro singers; (c), (f), (g) and (j), from notations of songs by white singers.

---

19. See Section 20, footnote 27.

Figure 25[20]

The last of the above examples exhibits in its second measure a type of off-beat singing not infrequently heard in Negro performance. See, for instance, the following measures from a Negro game song and three Negro spirituals.

---

20. The examples in Figures 25 and 26 are taken from the following songs: Figure 25, (a) *Adam in the Garden, Pinnin' Leaves*; (b) *The Blood-Strained Banders*; (c) *The Lexington Murder*; (d) *The Wind Blow East*; (e) *Trench Blues*; (f) *Low Down Lonesome Low*; (g) *Peter Gray*; (h) *God Moves on the Water*; (i) *Soon One Mornin', Death Come Creepin'*; (j) *Les Clefs de la Prison*. Figure 26 (a) *You Turn for Sugar and Tea*; (b) *If I Got My Ticket, Can I Ride?*; (c) *Low Down Chariot*, (d) [*Dem Bones*].

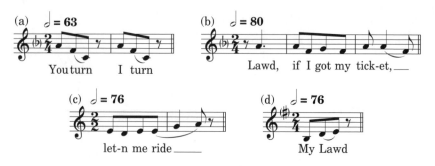

Figure 26[liii]

Related to the above practice is that shown in the following figures from *Mamma, Mamma*[liv] and *Pauline*:

Figure 27

It will be noted, in these, that the emphasis in the music is placed upon the weaker syllable in the text, a tendency frequently found in Negro singing.[21] A few further examples of this sort may not be out of place here. For, although at first sight they may appear to bear little (and, in (g) of Figure 28, no) relation to the subject of off-beat singing, it might be suggested as a point for discussion, that the displacement of the accustomed syllabic accent may be felt to contain a strong element of textual syncopation which cannot be dissociated from the music.

---

21. See also Henry Edward Krehbiel, *Afro-American Folksongs* (New York and London: G. Schirmer, 1914), [94–95].

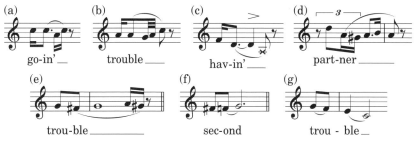

Figure 28[22]

20. Simple and compound meter

One difficulty in the transcription of folk songs into the notation of fine-art music is the long standing ambiguity in fine-art practice of the concept of measure. One and the same sequence of tone durations and accents can be written in several different ways, and the final choice is often highly subjective. Conversely, one and the same notation can be given such diverse readings by brilliant virtuosi as to throw considerable doubt upon the original intent of the composer. It can be said, however, that, although a few of the recordings from which these songs have been transcribed admit of wide and largely subjective choice in the selection of meter, the great majority of them present fairly obvious metrical patterns.

It has been customary for many years to determine and to notate the size of the measure in such a way as to show most clearly the symmetry and asymmetry of the metrical units or patterns. Thus, songs like *Where Have You Been, My Good Old Man?* and *John Henry* might have been given metrical signatures of 4/4, and written as follows:

Figure 29

22. The examples are taken from the following songs: (a) and (b) *Pauline*; (c) *Mamma, Mamma*; (d) *Lights in the Quarters, Burnin' Mighty Dim*; (e), (f) and (g) *Trouble, Trouble*.

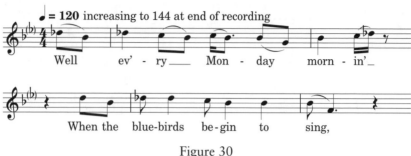

Figure 30

Such notation does not, however, give a true accentual picture of these songs as heard on the recordings. Indeed, it is highly misleading. For notation in 4/4 suggests some such differentiation of stress as 𝄽 𝄽 𝄽 𝄽,[23] and a resultant relaxed quality in the singing. The recordings of those two songs, on the other hand, show undifferentiated major stress—at the quarter-note units in *Where Have You Been, My Good Old Man?*, and at the half-note units in *John Henry*—which would appear to be most clearly indicated in the following less conventional manners:

Figure 31

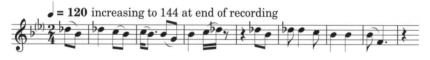

Figure 32

Similar distinctions can be made with respect to the use of a metrical signature of 6/8 as compared with that of 3/8. The first of these two meters is rarely heard on these recordings. *Billy Barlow,* below, provides a typical example. Metrical accents on the recording point indubitably to the signature of 3/8.

---

23. See Guido Adler, [?].[lv]

Figure 33

Such frequent recurrence of major stress as that heard in *Where Have You Been, My Good Old Man?* may be said to be the exception rather than the rule among these recordings. That heard in *John Henry* and in *Billy Barlow,*[lvi] however, is more or less typical of many, if not of a majority of them. Simple meters (1/8, 1/4, 1/2, 2/8, 2/4, 3/8, 3/2) are heard far more frequently than compound (4/8, 4/4, 4/2, 6/8, 6/4, 6/2, 9/8, 9/4, 9/2, 12/8, 12/4, 12/2 and other less usual) meters. Metrical accents are usually strong and undeniable, with added emphasis occasionally supplied by foot-tapping, clapping, chopping, tamping, and by accompanying instruments such as the guitar and banjo.

It has been felt to be self-evident, therefore, that clear indication of frequency in recurrence of major stress is of greater importance in the metrical notation of the singing of these songs, than is indication of symmetry and asymmetry of larger metrical patterns. It will be noted, in addition, that the smaller metrical signatures thus used are not only in most cases easier to read, but can allow inclusion, within the metrical frame, of occasional characteristic prolongations of tone or of rest which, had the song been notated in the larger meter, could not have been included without a change in metrical signature or the use of extra symbols (compare, for instance, Figures 29 and 31).

In notating meters, for the use of the general reader, which would most accurately be represented by metrical signatures of 1/4, 1/2, or 1/3, compromise has been felt to be advisable, in all but a few cases, with the less unusual metrical signatures of 2/8, 2/4, 3/8 and 3/4, since few people—indeed, few musicians—are comfortable when dealing with one beat per measure. In such cases, as has been pointed out in Section 18, the note-value employed as unit of measurement of the metronomic speed, at the heading of the song, will be found to be the guide as to the size of the metrical unit. Thus, in Figures 34 and 35, (a) should be understood to have been sung in metrical units of one (1/2); (b), in metrical units of two (2/4).

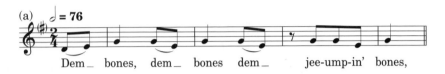

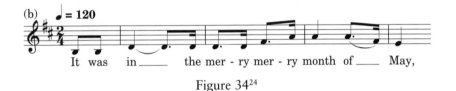

Figure 34[24]

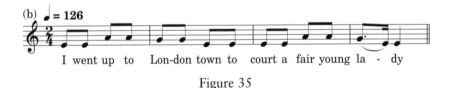

Figure 35

Since meters of 1/2, 2/4, and 2/2 are found to predominate among these recordings, a few further illustrations, of varying types, may not be out of place.

---

24. The examples are taken from the following songs: Figure 34, (a) *Dem Bones*; (b) *Sweet William*; Figure 35, (a) *Samson*; (b) *Devilish Mary*.

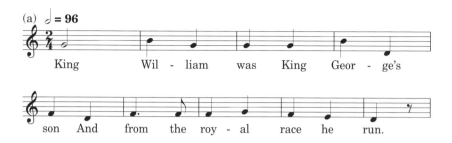

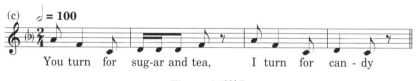

Figure 36[25,lvii]

Figure 37

25. Illustrations in Figures 36, 37 and 38 are taken from the following songs: Figure 36, (a) *King William Was King George's Son*; (b) *God Don't Like It*; (c) *You Turn for Sugar and Tea*. Figure 37, *O Lawd, I Went Up on the Mountain*; (b) *The Frenchman's Ball*; (c) *Toll-a-Winker*. Figure 38, (a) *When de Whale Gets Strike*; (b) *Adam in the Garden, Pinnin' Leaves*; (c) *Duncan and Brady*.

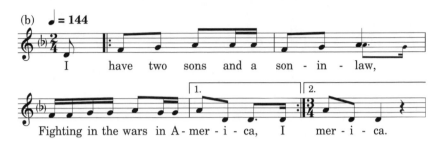

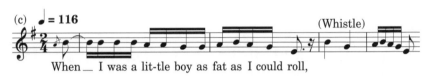

Figure 37 *(continued)*

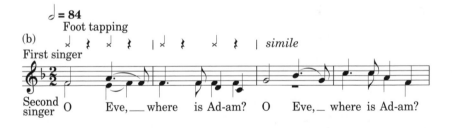

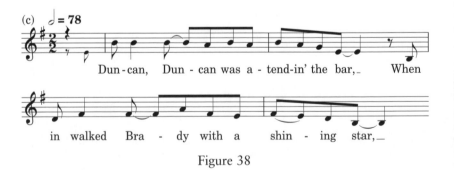

Figure 38

Illustration[lviii] of a few songs in triple meter may also be of interest.

Figure 39[26]

___
26. The illustrations are taken from the following songs: (a) *The Lady Who Loved a Swine*; (b) *Tee Roo*; (c) *Little Bonny*; (d) *Katy Dorey*; (e) *My Old True Love*.

The infrequent appearance of 4/4 meter on these recordings has already been noted. *Darling Corey, Do Come Back Again* and *Big Fat Woman* are among the comparatively few songs which have been felt to show in their singing unmistakable characteristics of this meter.

Wake up, wake up darl-ing Co-rey,——What makes you sleep so sound?

Once I knew a lit-tle girl and I loved her as — my — life;

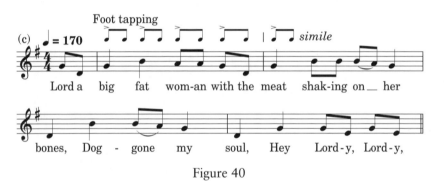

Lord a big fat wom-an with the meat shak-ing on — her

bones, Dog - gone my soul, Hey Lord-y, Lord-y,

Figure 40

Large phraseological 4/4 (or 4/2 or 4/1) and 3/4 (or 3/2 or 3/1, or 9/4 or 9/2) can, of course, not infrequently be heard. But here, even more than in such cases as are illustrated in Figures 29 to 32, the notation in the smaller units appears to be equally (if not more) correct, and certainly easier to read. See, for instance, *Little Willie's My Darling*:

Lit-tle Wil-lie's my dar - ling Lit-tle Wil-lie's my dear —

Figure 41

Noteworthy examples of large phraseological 4/4 can be found among the Negro work songs. For consistency in treatment of this group of songs as a whole, a few work songs which show strong major stress at the smaller metrical units have, nevertheless, been notated according to the larger metrical pattern. Thus, in *Lord, It's All, Almost Done* and *Don't Talk About It*,[27] although major stress suggests signature of 1/4, that of 4/4 has been used.[28] Clear indication, in this manner, of the larger metrical pattern has been felt to be of paramount importance in presentation of these songs as a group, in order that a clear picture may be given of the relation shown by the "work accents" to the metrical frame of which they form a part. For the recurrent breath expulsion ("huh"), and the beat of the axe or other instrument, would appear to be an essential if not a basic element in the metrical structure of this type of Negro work song as heard on these recordings. It may be of interest, in this connection, to note, in Figure 42,[lix] similarities in the metrical structure of songs (a), (f), (i) and (j), in which the work accent may be said to be implied though not present on the recording, and songs (b), (c), (d), (e), (g) and (h), in which the work accents are clearly heard.

[Figure 42, not extant]

It was with a view to such comparison of likenesses, and of differences, in metrical structure among work songs of this type, that the chart in Figure 42 was compiled. It includes all the Negro work songs, in the work song section of this[lx] collection of transcriptions, in which the work accent is either heard or felt to be implied. The three omitted work songs are of lyrical character. Songs (i) and (j) were dictated by intermediaries; all other songs were transcribed from field recordings. The chart should not be understood to imply any generalisations concerning Negro work songs outside this collection of transcriptions. The fact the eight songs transcribed from recordings were recorded in seven states may give added interest to similarities in structure.[29]

---

27. See (g) and (h) in Figure 42. See also (e), in which the recurrence of major stress at the smaller units was felt to be so persistent that its loss, through use of larger meter, would involve a basic change in the character of the song.

28. It will be noted, in the chart in Figure 42, that, in accordance with the practice set forth in Section 18, for use among this collection of transcriptions as a whole, the metronomic speed of all the work songs shown in the chart would point to the use of 4/2 rather than 4/4 meter. Exception has been allowed in these cases upon the basis of the accepted fact that 4/2 is a meter both unaccustomed and difficult to follow.

29. The songs illustrated in Figure 42, together with the state in which each was recorded, are as follows: (a) *Look Down that Lonesome Road*, South Carolina; (b)

Examples[lxii] should not be omitted of a few less-accustomed meters and alternations of meters heard on the recordings. The following examples are taken from songs in which such meters are more or less consistently maintained from stanza to stanza throughout the recording. Perhaps the most outstanding is that heard throughout the singing of the Cajun song *Belle,* which appears to be most accurately notated as 10/8 (see Figure 10).

The strongly accented and undeniable 5/4 of *Drop 'em Down,*[30,lxiii] and the 9/8 of *Ain't Workin' Song,*[lxiv] may be felt to partake of the nature of metrical curiosities, especially when viewed in relation to meters usually encountered in the singing of Negro work songs.

Figure 43

Figure 44

Take This Hammer, Virginia; (c) *Didn' Ol' John Cross the Water on His Knees?,* South Carolina; (d) *Pauline,* Tennessee; (e) *Drive It On,* Arkansas; (f) *You Kicked and Stomped and Beat Me,* Mississippi; (g) *Lord, It's Almost Done,* Alabama; (h) *Don't Talk About It,* North Carolina. The songs dictated by intermediaries are as follows: (i) *I Got to Roll,* heard in Tennessee; (j) *Godamighty Drag,*[lxi] heard in Texas.

30. This song was not included in final publication of *This Singing Country.* Its pertinence to the above discussion is felt, nevertheless, to warrant its inclusion here.

Notable illustration of alternation of meters can be heard throughout the singing of the many stanzas and choruses of *Roll On, Babe*, as also of the several repetitions of the stanza of *Little Bird, Go Through My Window*. In the former, the *patterns* of alternation exhibit a considerable amount of interstanzaic variation. In the latter, variation in phrase occurrence of the eighth rest (interpolated, it would seem, for intake of breath) provides the principal interstanzaic variation with respect to meter.

Figure 45

Figure 46

The metrical notations shown in the above four examples are those used in final publication of the songs. It might be of interest, in presenting one further example (taken from the chorus of *Choose You a Seat 'n' Set Down*[lxv]), to include two types of transcription. Type B was chosen for publication. The *pattern* of metrical alternation is maintained almost without change through the four recurrences which comprise each singing of the chorus, as well as throughout all repetitions of the chorus.

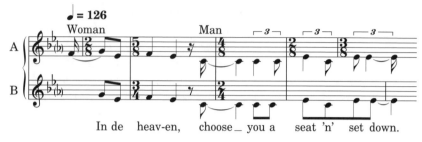

Figure 47

Each of the notations in Figures 43 to 47, as also in songs in more regular meters, can be said to represent more or less accurately the *individual metrical norm* felt to have been established in this particular singing of this particular song as a whole. With respect to any one of these examples, there can be seen to arise the question of relationships between this individual metrical norm and the individual metrical norms established by other singers in the singing of this tune and of related tunes within the same tune-family, existent over a specific period of time and within a coherent cultural unit. Comparison of a sufficient number of these individual metrical norms would allow determination of the nature of the *commonly possessed metrical norm* of that tune or tune-family. Determination of this commonly possessed metrical norm would allow the plotting of the degree of variation practiced in each case by the various singers, and would give grounds upon which to evaluate the tendency, common in the transcription and music-editing of folk songs, to throw the notation of the song into a regular or more accustomed metrical pattern—as, for instance, the 10/8 of *Belle* into a 2/4 or a 3/4 (see again, Figure 10), or the 5/4 of *Drop 'em Down* into a 4/4

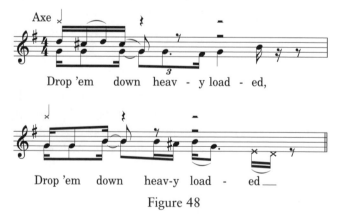

Figure 48

or the 9/8 of *Ain't Workin' Song* into a 2/2[31]

Figure 49

---

31. In spite of the fact that it is less accurate, this notation in 2/2 meter (as in Figure 49)—casting the song, as it does, in what may be felt to be a "typical" syncopated form—may on first consideration appear to give a more representative picture of the singing of the first stanza (and of the seven stanzas which follow) than does the notation in 9/8 (as in Figure 44).

Stanza 9, however, appears to be a strong deciding factor in this choice, and to point unquestionably to the advisability of notation in 9/8.

In measure 3 of stanza 9, the broken rhythms of the preceding stanzas give way to a series of strongly accented, insistent and regularly constructed figures, concerning whose notation there can be little doubt. The effect given is that of a slight increase in tempo.

If a meter of 2/2 is adopted for use in stanza 1, stanza 9 will then appear as follows:

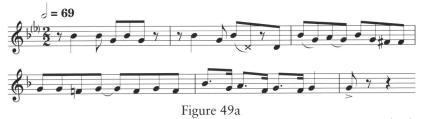

Figure 49a

Direct correspondence between equivalent note-values (i.e., a relationship of ♪ = ♪, ♩ = ♩, 𝅗𝅥 = 𝅗𝅥, etc.) is, obviously, implied in the above notation: the 8th-note value in measures 3, 4, and 5, for example, is understood to have been sung at the same metronomic speed as that in measures 1 and 2.

This is, however, not in accordance with the singing of this stanza as heard on the recording. Taking as a metronomic unit the 8th-note value in measure 3, it is found that this unit stands in the relationship of ♪ = ♪ to the 8th-note value in measures 1 and 2 *not* when they are notated in 2/2 meter (as in Figure 49a above) but when they are notated in 9/8 meter (as in Figure 49b below).

Figure 49b

or a continuous 2/4 as in *Roll On, Babe*[lxvi]

Figure 50

or a continuous 2/8 in *Little Bird, Go Through My Window*

Figure 51

or a continuous 2/4 in *Choose You a Seat 'n' Set Down.*

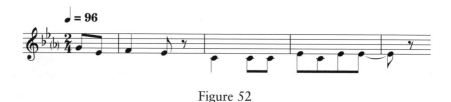

Figure 52

21. Metrical irregularities—prolongation and contraction of measure[lxvii]

Metrical irregularities of the sort illustrated in Figures 41 to 45, are comparatively rare on these recordings. The greater number of singers exhibit in their singing a basic regularity of pulse and meter which is maintained consistently enough throughout the singing of the song to be felt to represent its individual metrical norm. Within such norms, singers exhibit varying degrees of freedom. Occasional departures from the norm which can be notated as prolongation and contraction of measure, are not infrequent. They are followed, in most cases, by return to the norm.

It is a question, of course, whether the term "departure" should be used. If used, it is further a question as to when a particular "irregularity" may be felt to partake of the nature of a departure, and when it can be considered, rather, as an integral part of the metrical structure of the song. For departure from the metrical norm would seem at times to build, upon a higher level, a phrase and gross-form metrical norm whose recognition and notation may be as important to a full understanding of the music as are the details of measures and fractions of measures. Constant appearance of the metrical irregularity from stanza to stanza, together with invariability of tonal and rhythmic structure, would be principal determining factors in this building up of more elaborate concepts of phrase and gross-form metrical norm.

Prolongation and contraction of measure will be noted most frequently in these transcriptions at the breathing places in the song[lxviii]— the singer either increasing or decreasing the moment between the end of one phrase (or, occasionally, section[lxix]) and the beginning of another. An established norm of 2/4 may, for instance, be felt to be momentarily contracted to a 1/4 or prolonged to a 3/4, as in *Po' Laz'us* and *Lolly Too-Dum*.[lxx]

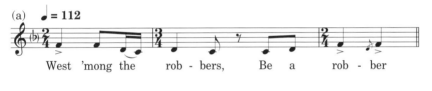

Figures 53a and 53b

A 3/4 may be momentarily contracted to 2/4,[lxxi] as in *Johnny Stiles*,

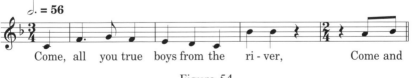

Figure 54

or prolonged to a 4/4 or a 5/4, as in *Tee Roo* and *The Irish Lady*.

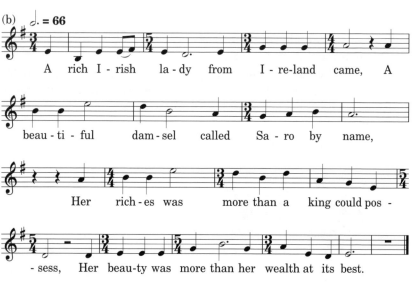

Figures 55a and 55b

Prolongation or contraction of an established measure-length *within the limits of the phrase* is not so frequently heard on these recordings, but is by no means rare. A single example may suffice, as representative of a considerable number of others. It is taken from *I Came to This Country in 1865.*[lxxii]

Figure 56[lxxiii]

Groups of songs which show the least metrical irregularity through prolongation or contraction of tone or rest, are the breakdowns and fiddle tunes, and the Negro spirituals, game songs and Bahaman[lxxiv] songs.

a. Prolongation of measure—the extended tone and the extended or inserted rest

As noted above, departure from a metrical norm which may be felt to be of the nature of prolongation of measure, is heard more frequently on these recordings than is departure which may be felt to be of the nature of contraction of measure.

The singers are found to expand the metrical norm:

(1) by interpolation of extra, separately enunciated tones to care for extra syllables in the text;
(2) by extension of the length of one single tone, or by extension of the length (or by insertion) of rest.

The first of these is heard occasionally (see Section 26); the second, frequently.

In some songs, extended tones and extended or inserted rest show little or no interstanzaic variation, either in duration or in position within the stanza (as in the singing of *East Virginia* and *Texas Rangers*). In other songs—notably, those in rubato-parlando singing-style—their duration and position tends to differ with each stanza (as in the singing of *The Little Brown Bulls*). In between these extremes will be found many songs in which constancy of duration and of position within the stanza is heard in a majority of the stanzas (as in the singing of *The Irish Lady*).

In such songs as *The Little Brown Bulls,* variation in position of extended tones and extended or inserted rest is found to be of two kinds:

(1) variation with respect to position *within the phrase* (i.e., whether occurring in measure 1, and/or measure 2, and/or measure 3, and/or measure 4, etc.)
(2) variation with respect to position *within the stanza* (i.e., whether occurring in phrase 1, and/or phrase 2, and/or phrase 3, and/or phrase 4, etc.).

Occurrence of the metrical irregularity in all phrases of a stanza, and/or in parallel measure-position within each phrase of that stanza, is rare on these recordings.

Since (1) and (2) above seldom combine to form an unvarying pattern of occurrence from stanza to stanza throughout the song, a third sort of variation may be seen to arise from their interplay:

(3) interstanzaic variation with respect to combination of the pattern of occurrences within any one stanza, as compared with that found within any other one stanza.

The general impression given by the complex relations established between such interstanzaic variations as these is not one of promiscuity.[lxxv] It would seem, in fact, that comparative studies of these variations might well disclose a balance of symmetry in the interplay of relative duration, frequency of occurrence and position within measure, stanza and song as a whole.

b. Underlimit of metrical irregularity shown in these notations, especially with regard to extension of tone and extension or insertion of rest

In determining the underlimit of metrical irregularity to be included in his notations, the transcriber must again consider the ultimate use to which his transcriptions will be put. For scientific study, all rhythmic and metrical details will be notated with minute precision, and consequently the exact length of extended tone and of extended or inserted rest will be indicated down to fractions of beats. For school or community use, such irregularities are customarily omitted entirely; extension of tone, when included at all, is loosely indicated as a hold of indefinite length (fermata), and few distinctions are made between the extended tone and extended or inserted rest.

In working with this collection of songs it was felt that, again here, a course midway between the extremes could be plotted, which would give a sound basis for appreciation and understanding of this important aspect of rhythmic style in folk singing, yet would preserve the simplicity necessary to sight-reading. In pursuit of this objective, the beat was chosen as the underlimit of metrical irregularity to be included in the notation of a majority of the songs, and likewise as the unit of measurement in notation of extended tone or rest whose length is greater than the beat. The aim has been:

(1) to include prolongation and contraction of measure of the length of one beat or more, in moderate, moderately fast or fast tempo (i.e., of the length of an 8th note in 2/8, 3/8, 4/8 meter, etc., of a quarter-note in 2/4, 3/4, 4/4, etc., and, by exception, of a quarter-note in 1/2, 2/2, 3/2, etc.);

(2) when the metrical irregularity is of the nature of extended tone or of extended or inserted rest, to notate it in definite rather than indefinite time-values, with the pulse as unit of measurement.

Realization of this aim, without too great complexity in notation, has been felt to be possible in well over a majority of the songs.

c. Manners of notating extended tone and extended or inserted rest

Since extended tones and extended or inserted rest occur with considerable frequency, their inclusion by change of metrical signature would greatly complicate the appearance of the notations, and so preclude the singing of many songs by many readers. The simple metrical outline has, therefore, in most cases been preserved, and these irregularities have been notated by means of two familiar symbols given definite rather than their customary indefinite durations.[lxxvi]

indicates that a second beat, of the value of the denominator of the metrical signature, should be added to the tone over which the sign appears. Thus (as in *The Wild Colonial Boy*):

Figure 57

indicates that a second and third beat, each of the value of the denominator of the metrical signature, should be added to the tone over which the sign appears. Thus (as in *The Little Brown Bulls*):

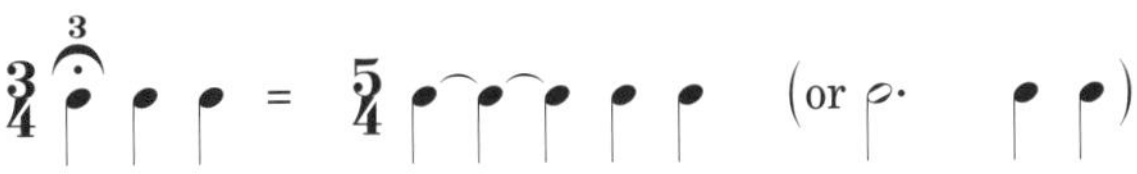

Figure 58

or (as in *Texas Rangers*).[lxxvii]

Figure 59

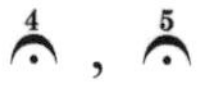

$\overset{4}{\frown}$, $\overset{5}{\frown}$, etc.[lxxviii]

should be interpreted accordingly.

,

indicates that one beat of rest, of the value of the denominator of the metrical signature, should be added or interpolated. Thus (as in *My Father Gave Me a Lump of Gold*):

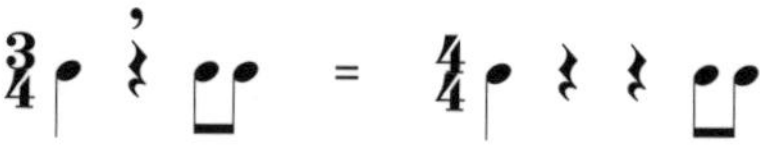

Figure 60

or (as in *The Irish Lady*)

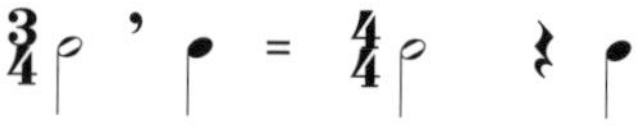

Figure 61

and " [lxxix] should be interpreted accordingly.

   Some irregularities which have been noted to occur with especial consistency throughout the singing of the song as a whole, or whose notation by the above means proved impractical, have been entered by change of metrical signature. See, for instance, the following measures from *Ox Driving Song*:

Figure 62[lxxx]

In a few songs, indication by either of the above means appeared impractical to simple notation, and footnotes have been appended (as in *Johnny Stiles, The Blood-Strained Banders,*[lxxxi] and *Soon One Mornin', Death Come Creepin'*).[lxxxii]

22. Metrical irregularities—divisions of beat and measure

Folk singers habitually divide beats and measures in characteristic and often highly irregular ways, some of which exhibit peculiarly elusive forms of rubato. Some of these are simple enough to be allowed inclusion in a singing book of this sort; many were, of necessity, excluded.

One of these practices—namely, unequal division of beat—deserves special mention here. There are few songs which do not show instances of it in its simplest form—the uneven triplet. It is so frequently heard, in fact, that rather than clutter up the page with a mass of indications such as ⌐³⌐ and ⌐⁵⌐, advantage has been taken, regretfully, of the convention common in both popular and fine-art music, of writing these unequal divisions in the simpler way and relying for proper performance upon the reader's familiarity with current practice. According to this convention, such figures as ♪. ♪, ♩. ♪, ♪ ♪, ♪ ♩. are often performed as ♩♩, ♩♩, ♪♪, ♩♩; and ♪ ♩ ♪ as ♪ ♩. ♪. Current practice in the performance of such figures is found to vary according to tempo of performance. Thus, in fast time, ♪. ♪ is almost invariably ♩♩, while in slow time the same figure may be sung as written, or frequently as ♩♪.[lxxxiii]

Another practice deserving of mention is the alternate use of the triplet and duplet form within the same song (as in the recording of *The Rowan County Crew*). Some stanzas can be felt to show meter of 2/4, others of 6/8, while still others show varying degrees of alternation between the two meters within the limits of a single stanza.

The most elusive examples of rhythmic irregularity—the more complex of the Negro hollers—have purposely been omitted from this collection of songs. The relative simplicity of those which have been considered simple enough to include may give an idea of the complexity of those omitted.[32,lxxxiv]

23. Rest[lxxxv]

Silence, or rest, is an integral part of the artistry of singing.[lxxxvi] It is a question whether, in the transcribing and notating of a song and its singing, accuracy in indication of rest-durations may not be of as nearly great importance as accuracy in indication of relative tone-durations. Certainly, considerations of rest with respect to what may be felt to be its most outstanding function, that of punctuation—and the drawing of musical and literary analogies with respect to this function—would in itself urge care in the notation of rest-duration, at phrase- and stanza-ends as well as within the phrase.

Rest is most frequently heard at phrase- and stanza-end, at which points there is generally apparent on the recording an intake of breath. Less frequent—but by no means uncommon—is rest within the limits of the phrase, with no intake of breath apparent on the recording. In either case, the rest may or may not involve prolongation of an established meter. Such prolongation is, however, more often coincident with the breath intake. In transcription of these songs, it has been felt that distinction between amounts of rests which involve no change of established meter—as, for instance, in measure 4 of *My Father Gave Me a Lump of Gold*

Figure 63[lxxxvii]

---

32. See, for instance, *Trouble, Trouble*; *Make Me a Garment*; *Lights in the Quarter Burnin' Mighty Dim*, as well as the work song *Pauline*.

should receive as close consideration as the more outstanding ex-amples of rest which involve such change.[lxxxviii]

It has been noted on these recordings that most singers, when unac-companied, continue from stanza to stanza with little (and, in some cases, with no) break in the flow of the song as a whole. The amounts of rest allowed between the stanzas of any one song can, in a majority of cases, be felt to be as consistent an element in the singing of the song as a whole as are those amounts of rest allowed within any one single stanza. Interstanzaic rest-duration has, therefore, received as careful attention in transcription of these songs as have rest-durations within the stanza. Accordingly, the amount of rest (or, occasionally, absence of rest) heard at the end of the stanza has, with a few exceptions, been indicated in the notation (,[lxxxix] or, in a few instances, by means of a footnote in the notation, as in *The Blood-Strained Banders* and *Johnny Stiles*).[xc] In accompanied songs, the durations of the longer interstanzaic rest-durations allowed during instrumental interludes have, for obvious reasons, not been notated. Some of these are discussed in Section 30.

Absence of indication of rest in the notation signifies that no break in the sound-stream was audible on the recording. Such songs as *Pay Day at Coal Creek*, with the entire stanza apparently sung in one breath, are rare in this collection.

24. Phrase pattern

a. Number of measures to a phrase[xci]

Obviously, any comprehensive study of phrase-lengths should be made upon the basis of acquaintance with all stanzas of the song, since any one phrase, recurrent from stanza to stanza throughout the song, may show interstanzaic variation in length. In such a study, distinction will be made between:

(1) phrase irregularities which appear to have been more or less required by irregularity in the text
(2) phrase irregularities which appear to be of purely musical na-ture—as, for instance, musical ornamentation of single syl-lables (see Figure 8) or extension of tone or rest.

Distinction would also be made between accompanied and unac-companied songs, since singers, when accompanied, tend to allow an occasional measure or more for instrumental interlude.

Such a study of these songs has not been made. But it can be stated that, as sung from beginning to end, well over half of them show a predominantly two- or four-measure phrase-pattern. Phrases showing other patterns have, in many cases, been found to contain extension of tone and/or rest which, if shortened or omitted, could conceivably permit phrase analysis within a two- or four-measure pattern. The Negro hollers form the chief exception. The question of phrase-norm which obviously arises here can be seen to be closely connected to that of metrical norm: namely, to what extent, in the singing of any one song, can irregularity in phrase-length be said to be representative of "the song," and to what extent, of its singing?

b. Number of phrases to the [stanza][xcii]

About two-thirds of the songs in this collection exhibit two or four phrases to the stanza; a sixth, three phrases; a scattered dozen, five phrases. The remainder are too diverse in type to admit of discussion here.

Consideration of the three- and five-phrase stanzas with respect to textual pattern reveals that, with a few rare exceptions (such as that found in *Do Come Back Again* and in *Don't You Like It?*) the odd phrase is of the nature of:

(1) a refrain (as in *Katy Dorey, Harvey Logan* and others)
(2) a textual repeat of a first line (as in *Pretty Polly,*[xciii] *Chilly Winds, Po' Laz'us* and others) or of a last line (as in *John Henry, Blue Bottle, When de Whale Get Strike*[xciv] and others).

In the latter case (2), the music to which the repeated line is sung is seldom the same in both phrases. Varying degrees of likeness will be heard, from the slight variation in *Blue Bottle* or *Po' Laz'us* to the more extensive differences in *Chilly Winds*.

Mention should not be omitted of the tendency shown among the "blues"[xcv] to be cast in a three-phrase pattern (as in *I Been a Bad, Bad Girl, I'm Worried Now But I Won't Be Worried Long, I'm a Stranger Here* and others).[xcvi]

25. Interstanzaic variation[xcvii]

The factor of interstanzaic variation is, as can be seen, closely interwoven with all other factors in the singing of folk songs. Most

of the observations made throughout these pages can be said, therefore, to be concerned either directly or indirectly with this factor. It is
hoped that at some time in the future a more comprehensive study
can be made of this subject.

Since the rhythm of the words is a strong determining element[xcviii]
in the rhythmic contour of a folk song, it is not surprising to note
that rhythmic interstanzaic variation is more frequently encountered[xcix] in these songs than tonal. Even without (or with slight) change
of stress in the words of various stanzas, and in the simpler singing
styles, it is constantly in evidence[c] (see, for instance, measure 3 of
The Raving Shanty Boy[ci] given below).

Figure 64 [*The Raving Shanty Boy*][cii]

Interstanzaic variations from the recording of *Oh, Roll On, Babe*
may be of interest as an example of both tonal and rhythmic change
from stanza to stanza. They exhibit a degree of variation about midway in complexity between that of a holler like *Trouble, Trouble*

and a song like *Washington the Great*[ciii] (whose chief interstanzaic variation consists in the changing position, in relation to the principle tones of the tune, occupied by an occasional quick accented or unaccented slide).

Figure 65 [*Oh, Roll On, Babe* variations, not extant][civ]

26. Manners of accommodating extra syllables of succeeding stanzas[cv]

Singers show several methods of accommodating to the rhythmic patterns of the music the occasional extra syllables which occur in the text. In some cases these syllables will be crowded into the established metrical pattern, the total measure-length remaining unchanged. In others an added beat or more will be inserted to care for the extra syllables in more leisurely fashion. In both instances the pitch on which the added syllables are sung is quite likely to remain that of the tone which precedes their insertion (as in *The "Bigler"*). In rarer instances the extra words or lines of text become an occasion for more varied musical departures, based tonally on material already sung, but varied rhythmically according to the added words. Especially clear illustration of this practice can be heard in the recordings of *Les Clefs de la Prison*[cvi] and *Roustabout Holler,* complete transcriptions of which could not be published for lack of space.

27. Tone attack and release[cvii]

Folk singers employ to varying extents melodic ornaments elusive to the professional mind and ear, but essential elements of the idiom in which they sing.[33,cviii] Of the simpler ornaments, probably the most characteristic and easily described are those which attend and modify the attack and the release of a tone.

a. Attack

The longer tones of a tune are often preceded by quick slides. When the singer gives these slides the accent which normally would

---

33. William Francis Allen's much quoted reference to "slides from one note to another, and turns and cadences not in articulated notes" could be applied as well to a considerable degree of white singing. (William Francis Allen, *Slave Songs of the United States* [New York: Peter Smith, 1867, new edition 1929], v, vi.)[cix]

be given the longer tone which they precede, they are in most cases felt to be part of the metrical frame and have been written into the notation as such (see, for instance, *Little Bonny* or *Diamond Joe*).[cx] When they are unaccented, the longer tone is usually found to have been given its full value, and the preceding ornament has been written outside the metrical frame as a grace-note (see *The Sporting Cowboy* or *Au Long de ce Rivage*).[cxi] In some songs the distinction between the accented and the unaccented slide is made especially apparent through the appearance of both within the same stanza (see *Belle* or *As I Set Down to Play Tin-can*).[cxii]

b. Release

Manners of tone release are many.[cxiii] They include, among others, the half-sung, half-spoken drop of the voice so characteristic of Negro singing (see *Samson*) and the quick upward flip heard frequently among both white and Negro singers. The pitch of these final tones is sometimes definite enough to allow their inclusion in customary notation. At other times they are indicated by the symbol $\downarrow$. Both means of indication have been used in *John Done Saw That Number*.

A tone release of a different sort is the "huh!" of the Negro work song. This is described by Alan Lomax as a more or less violent expulsion of the breath from the body, occurring at the moment when the axe hits the tree (or at the instant of contact, whatever instrument is in use). It is a form of exclamation, indicating that the effort has reached its climax.

28. Intonation[cxiv]

Professional and amateur fine-art musicians are often heard to say that folk musicians sing "out-of-tune." It is quite true, they do often sing out of tune with the equal-tempered scale of the pianoforte, as do also professional and amateur fine-art musicians,[34] though probably in different ways. The "breadth" (variation of intonation)[35] of each tone in the equal-tempered scale, and the occasions upon

---

34. See Otto Abraham and E.M. von Hornbostel, "Tonometrische Untersuchungen an einem deutschen Volkslied," *Psychologische Forschung* 4 (1923): 1–22.

35. See Joseph A. Yasser, *A Theory of Evolving Tonality*, American Library of Musicology (New York: Norton, 1932), 56 n.[cxv]

which advantage may be taken of it, have been fairly established by tradition. In order to judge whether a tone is in or out of tune in fine-art practice, it has been necessary to have determined to a certain degree of accuracy the intonation of a scale to which it could be referable, and to be able to perceive the "breadths" of the degrees allowed in this scale by the best practice. There is no reason to expect the folk musician to follow fine-art tradition when he has, apparently, folk-art traditions of his own no less old and legitimate. Comprehensive acoustical measurements of the tonal materials of American folk music have not been made. We cannot, therefore, at this time determine what the norms may be, what is their geographic distribution, or what degree of variation from them is approved by the best folk practice.

Among the songs in this volume, the most marked tonal deviations from fine-art practice are the tones popularly called "blue notes," found in the recordings of both white and Negro singers. Their focus may most often be plotted between and around major and minor scale degrees[36]—mainly those of the 3rd and 7th.[37] Some of the more stable of these characteristic intonations define a pitch roughly midway between the major and the minor 3rd and the major and minor 7th—the so-called "neutral" 3rd and 7th.[38] Others approximate closely the major norm; still others, the minor.

---

36. In his Preface to the 1877 edition of *Cabin and Plantation Songs* (New York: G.P. Putnam), Thomas P. Fenner speaks of such tones as "ranging through an entire interval on different occasions." See also Winthrop Sargeant, "The Scalar Structure of Jazz," in *Jazz: Hot and Hybrid,* ed. Winthrop Sargeant (New York: Arrow Editions, 1938).

37. See also the flat 5th in such songs as *If I Got My Ticket, Can I Ride?*; *I Been a Bad, Bad Girl*; *Mamma, Mamma*; and *Make Me a Garment*; the flat 2nd in *The Rich Old Lady*; and the raised 4th in *The Blood-Strained Banders*; *God Don't Like It*; and *Pretty Polly*. (See Sargeant, ed., *Jazz: Hot and Hybrid*). A few singers show the tendency to substitute for the major 6th degree (as for instance, A in the key of C) a tone approximating the augmented 6th degree (as A♯ in the key of C) close enough to be notated. This usually occurs in progression from and back to a tonic above. Due to the difficulty of reading the resultant diminished 3rd (A♯ to C) the enharmonic minor 7th degree (as B♭) has been used in these notations. In some cases this (written) minor 7th may thus be said to have two functions within the same song (see the D♭ in *John Done Saw That Number.*).

38. Ellis, in that part of the appendix to Helmholtz' *On the Sensations of Tone* in which he deals with certain non-European scales (Arabian, Indian, Japanese, and others), refers to "Neutral intervals, each lying between two European intervals, and having the character of neither, but serving for either, . . ." Herman von Helmholtz, *The Sensations of Tone as a Physiological Basis of Music,* 3rd ed. (London: Longmans, Green and Co., 1898), 525.

It has been noted that blue or neutral tones referable to any single scale-degree, and recurrent throughout a stanza or song, frequently exhibit varying degrees of "blueness." Sometimes these blue tones will vary within each stanza, or stanzas will vary one from the other with respect to such tones, or stanzas appearing nearer to major, another to minor, still another approximating a mid-point.[cxvi] It has been noted that a "blue effect" is often achieved by means of a rapid slide from one tone to another within a limited range, so that what may at first give the impression of a single blue note is in reality a complex of two, or of several (see *Prison Moan, Marthy Had a Baby, Hard Times in the Country, Trouble, Trouble,* and others). It has further been observed that two singers, singing the same tune simultaneously, may at certain points employ two levels of "blueness" (as in the recording of *Choose You a Seat 'n' Set Down*). With a larger group, such as that in *Go Down, Ol' Hannah* this heterophony is striking.[cxvii] Finally, in many recordings repeated hearing will reveal the fact that the blue notes do not stand apart from their fellows so much as at first seemed the case, the surrounding tones representing an imperceptibly graduated scale of departure from fine-art standards ranging from obviously "distorted" single intonations to such subtle nuances in the whole melodic line that only the laboratory instrument could distinguish them from orthodox fine-art practice.

Experience with this collection would indicate that the white singer makes almost as insistent use of the blue or neutral 3rd and/or 7th as does the Negro singer.[39] It is a question to what extent the varying pitch levels shown in their singing are effected by such factors as variation of melodic context (for instance, as approach from below and above), syllabification—whether rapid or slow— and so on.[cxviii]

29. Scale and mode[cxix]

Classification of a tune according to scale requires computation and analysis of the tonal aggregate of the whole song. Classification

---

39. Examples of Negro songs exhibiting blue or neutral 3rds and/or 7ths are: *John Done Saw That Number; God Moves on the Water; Adam in the Garden, Pinnin' Leaves; God Don't Like It; Po' Laz'us; Drive It On; Johnny Won't You Ramble?; Take This Hammer;* and *Lord, It's Almost Done*. Among the white songs are: *King William Was King George's Son; Keep Your Hands on That Plow; Hog Rogues on the Harricane; Greenland Whale Fishery; Pretty Polly; Blanche Comme la Neige; Les Clefs de la Prison; The Bachelor's Lay; The Raving Shanty Boy; The Reek and the Rambling Blade; The Vance Song;* and *Pass Around Your Bottle*.

is a scientific process and the task of the trained scholar, who will (as stated in [Sections 10 and 11])[cxx] require the tunes of all stanzas in making any generalizations regarding a song. Labelling of a model stanza according to scale may be misleading, since other stanzas may disclose addition or omission of tones essential to classification. Such labelling of a composite tune may, at best, be said to be open to question.[cxxi]

Classification of a tune according to mode requires at least
(a) computation and analysis of scalar material, and
(b) analysis of the functional relationship of the various elements in the tonal aggregate in respect to each other and to the whole of which they are parts—particularly as regards
(1) the sum-total time-values given to each degree of the scale established,[40]

---

40. Need for such analysis can clearly be seen through computation of the relative time-values within the model stanza of such a song as *Low Down Lonesome Low*:

Figure 66[cxxii]

(2) the relationships of phrase initials and finals,[41] and
(3) the tonal range in relation to the tonal center.

Occasional shifting of tonal center from stanza to stanza, as well as variability of intonation (especially on the 3rd and 7th degrees) should, in addition to the above points, advise utmost caution in classification by mode, and even by scale.

Clearly, the question, what is the scale or the mode of a folk song, is a controversial one. Further complication derives from the obvious fact that various transcribers, in notating the same song,[cxxiii] will render transcriptions of varying character and detail according to their various objectives.[cxxiv] Obviously, not all minute tonal phenomena can be considered in computation of scale—still less mode, which after all, is an ordering of the tonal aggregate of a song as a norm of general practice accepted by tradition.

The question is important, then: is a scale a grouping in order of pitch of all the elements in the tonal aggregate, or of only some of them; and if the latter, which? Is a mode merely a scale with a tonal center?

Upon the basis of these considerations and others—added to the fact that we do not ourselves know much about the inner organization of the "ecclesiastical" modes as distinguished from that of the modern major and minor modes—the Music Editor[cxxv] is inclined to question the emphasis placed in recent publications upon scalar and "modal" (i.e., "ecclesiastical-modal") characteristics in American folk songs. (It is, for instance, not clear why a song in C Major should be said to be in the Ionian mode only when it is a folk song). As Barry says, "Nothing in folk song is more evanescent than modality."[42] It would seem that more valuable, and certainly more scientific guides to tonal classification may be found in M. Kolinski's[cxxvi] analysis of

---

It should be noted that the A (time-value, one 16th) is a vital tone in classification of this tune according to prevailing "ecclesiastical-model" standards. It should further be pointed out that all stanzas but two omit the A entirely, a G being sung in its place.

41. See Béla Bartók, *Hungarian Folk Music,* trans. M. D. Calvocoressi (London: Oxford University Press, 1931).

42. Phillips Barry, "The Music of the Ballads," in *British Ballads from Maine,* ed. Phillips Barry, Fannie Hardy, and Mary Winslow Smyth (New Haven: Yale University Press, 1929), xxv–xxvi.

the Suriname songs,[43] and in Béla Bartók's classification of Hungarian folk songs.[44]

30. Accompaniment[cxxvii]

Of the 197 tunes transcribed[cxxviii] from these recordings, 46 were sung to accompaniment: 28 to guitar, 6 to [5–]string banjo,[cxxix] 2 to guitar and banjo, 2 to guitar and mandolin, 2 to string band (fiddle, guitar, banjo, mandolin, auto-harp) one to accordion, 2 to Bahaman drum, and 3 to Bahaman street band (mandolin, guitar, tenor banjo). Experience with these and similar recordings indicates the presence of a surprising amount of instrumental virtuosity in the land, though as yet little or no study has been made of it.

A good "folk" guitar technique usually includes, among other capacities, keeping the chords going fast and strong. Simple triads are most used, distinctively except in the "blues" technique. Major triads are preferred to minor. A minor tune may, in fact find itself accompanied in major.[cxxx]

The banjo is usually 5–stringed, the 5th string[cxxxi] acting as a high pedal-point and providing the listener with many rhythmic and tonal refinements. A banjo accompaniment may at first give the impression of being less closely bound than a guitar accompaniment to the tune it accompanies. Yet upon close analysis the banjo accompaniment will generally reveal the exact tones of the song, occurring on minute subdivisions of beats and surrounded by a mass of accessory tones.

The mandolin is more generally used in instrumental groups than its one[cxxxii] appearance on these recordings would indicate.

Fiddles appear only in company with other instruments on these recordings, when accompanying a song. In *Batson* they maintain a melodic line independent of the tune of the song, the guitar supplying the chordal basis. The string-band accompaniment to *Long Lonesome Road* also contains a distinctive fiddle figuration. An example of virtuosity in solo playing may be heard in *Callahan,*[cxxxiii] whose two simultaneous melodic lines are maintained by the one player at breakneck speed.

Fiddle and banjo players often change their tuning, according to the tune they are playing. Exceptional fiddlers may use as many as

---

43. Melville Herskovits, Frances Shapiro Herskovits, and Mieczyslaw Kolinski, *Suriname Folk-Lore,* Columbia University Contributions to Anthropology, 27 (New York: Columbia University Press, 1936).

44. Béla Bartók, *Hungarian Folk Music.*

Plate 7. Ruth Crawford Seeger's incomplete sketch for the transcription of the fiddle tune *Glory in the Meetin' House*. (Photo, Lomax [John Avery] Family Papers, Center for American History, University of Texas at Austin. Used by permission.)

eight tunings.[45] "Tuning up" can be as delicate an affair with the fiddle or banjo player as with the fine-art performer.

The accompaniment rarely stops from beginning to end of the song. It is the business of the accompanist(s) not only to keep going throughout each stanza, but to take up the slack during breathing spaces at phrase-ends, and at times to provide interludes between stanzas. Most interludes in the songs in this volume are fairly short, showing slight interstanzaic variation in length. These short interlude-lengths have been included in the notations—in the form either of rests (as in *Pretty Polly*) or of long held tones in the voice (as in *The White House Blues*). Inclusion of the longer interlude-lengths has appeared impractical.

It has been found that these longer interludes frequently take the form of figurations of the tune itself, and in many cases are more or less exact repetitions of the material used for accompaniment of the stanza.[cxxxiv] In guitar accompaniments they seldom appear after all stanzas of the song. The accompaniment to *The Sporting Cowboy*, for instance, after a prelude of 17 measures, gives interludes of 17 1/2 measures each[cxxxv] after stanzas 2 and 3, with short interludes of two measures and of one measure after stanzas 1 and 4 respectively, and a coda of 16 measures. In *Hard Times in the Country* the guitar and banjo accompaniment gives interludes of 24 measures after stanzas 2, 4, 6, and 7 (coda) with no interlude after the remaining stanzas. The string-band accompaniment to *Long Lonesome Road* gives interludes of 12 measures after stanzas 3, 5, and 9 (coda), with no interludes after the remaining stanzas.

Banjo accompaniments on these recordings (representing the work of four players from Kentucky, Virginia and Ohio) show more constant appearance of interludes between stanzas, and greater similarity in interlude-lengths. See, for instance, the accompaniment to *East Virginia*, with interludes to the extent of 18 beats after stanzas 1, 5, 7, and 9, and of 20 beats after stanzas 3, 4, 6, and 8—together with prelude to the extent of 18 beats, and coda (after stanza 10) of 14 beats; or the accompaniment to *Roll On, Babe*, with interlude to the extent of 11 beats after the first stanza and chorus, and of 12 beats after each succeeding stanza and chorus thereafter—together with prelude to the extent of 8 beats, and coda of 12 beats.

The Bahaman band accompaniments on these recordings comprise a prelude, accompaniment throughout the singing, and a coda, with interludes rarely breaking the repetitions of the stanzas. The drum no-

45. On the duplicate disc used for transcription of *Callahan*, the pitch is A. Since fiddle players are known to use the tunings G–D–G–D and A–E–A–E interchangeably, it is a question in this case which was used.

tated with *The Wind Blow East* and *Biddy, Biddy* exhibits several pitches; predominating pitches approximate V and I. The drum notation in each of these songs is that which accompanies the initial tune of the first stanza and chorus. Rhythms vary with each succeeding stanza, tending[cxxxvi] to become more complex and insistent as the song proceeds.[cxxxvii]

Plate 8. Members of the Midcentury International Folklore Society, held at Indiana University in July, 1950. Ruth Crawford Seeger, back row, next to last person, with Charles Seeger at the end of the row. Others (reading left to right) include George Herzog (row one, number six), Maud Karpeles (row one, number seven), Stith Thompson (row one, last person), and Sidney Robertson Cowell (row four, number five). They represent the intended professional audience for *The Music of American Folk Song*. (Photograph reproduced with permission from the Archives of Traditional Music, Indiana University.)

Plate 9. The Seeger family, ca. 1941: Charles, Peggy, Ruth, Barbara, Mike. (Photo, Seeger family. Used by permission.)

This Christmas card photograph was mailed to a friend later with the following note from Ruth: "Dear Dorothy, Believe it or not this card has been waiting a year to be sent with you. In the midst of sending my cards last year, arrived a very urgent deadline on the Lomax book, which made it necessary for me to tuck the remaining 25 cards in a drawer and tackle an exciting proof-reading job as a Christmas present. . . . As for me, I've been mostly recuperating from the night work (incessant) on the book. It is out now—*Our Singing Country*, Macmillan—and is a relief as well as a source of pleasure for the whole family. Barbara is in a cooperative nursery school; Peggy in first grade, Michael in third. . . ."

Plate 10. The Seeger family, ca. 1949–50: Mike, Barbara, Penny, Charles, Peggy, Ruth. (Photo, Seeger family. Used by permission.)

Editor's Notes

i. There are two first pages in β, numbered [1A] and [1B], with slightly different texts. [1B] contains pencilled-in commentary and a number of handwritten corrections. It is difficult to know which of these pages was written first, and which was intended as final. From the nature of the editing, it appears that [1B] is the later edition; it is used here. The significant difference is in b. and c. of the list of "characteristics." In [1A] they are:

b. While there is abundant evidence of application of the study of the idiom, this study appears not to be consciously regarded as [study,] such by the possessors of the idiom, but rather as the "learning of a song" or, occasionally, even of the "composing of a song"—this use of the word "composition" not being understood in the sense of the conventional use of the term among professional musicians.

c. This learning, in a vast majority of cases, appears to have been done with no other written technique than that of language, and in a very large majority of cases, even without this. The learning was thus, in the main, "by ear," and in conformity with prevailing oral traditions. It is reasonably certain that few could read or write any music notation, or that they learned the songs from singers who could read or write it.

"Remarks on Transcription" is written in β, "Table of Contents" page, but the two differing first pages have the section titles: "A Few Notes on Transcription" and "A Notes [sic] on Transcription" [1A]. α has the title "A Few Remarks on Transcription" on its first page of text. [1B] was probably intended to be "A Note on Transcription" [1B] and is the title of this section, used in this edition (note that this differs from the title used in Cardullo and Tick, who both refer to this section as titled "Remarks on Transcription").

ii. In the typescript there appears to be a typographical error, with the word "as" appearing where, I believe, the word "is" is intended.

iii. The word "therefore" is circled in light pencil and appears to have an editorial deletion mark connected to it. It is retained in this edition.

iv. *Po' Farmer* is on Rounder 1827, but it is unclear whether or not this is the recording used in *OSC*. RCS mentions that it was transcribed from a "commercial recording," but the version in *OSC* says: "No record. Negro share-cropper on the Smithers Plantation, Huntsville, Texas, 1934. Given by A. Lomax." In the notes to Rounder 1827 the song is attributed to Lemuel Jones, recorded by John Lomax on 5/31/36, and it is noted that "this song was printed in *OSC*."

v. This list also appears in RCS's "Music Preface" to *OSC*. *The High Barbaree* is also included in the "1001 Folksongs" Papers, but in a different version, and is called, on certain pages, *The Wild Barbaree* (Child 285). This version may be the one on AFS L21.

vi. Herzog, a leading and pioneering folksong scholar, was an important influence for RCS's ideas on transcription. The article quoted here was also printed as "Observations and Suggestions" in the *Southern Folklore Quarterly* 1 (June 1937): 25–27. Tick (pp. 245–46) discusses Herzog's association with the Lomaxes, and how their experience with his transcription methods might have led them to RCS. For more on this topic see Nolan Porterfield, *Last Cavalier: The Life and Times of John A. Lomax, 1867–1948* (Urbana: University of Illinois Press, 1996), 414–16. Some of Herzog's notational conventions, used in the Leadbelly book (as referenced in the "Music Preface" to *OSC*): J. A. Lomax and A. Lomax, *Negro Folk Songs As Sung by Lead Belly,* (New York: Macmillan, 1934), may have influenced RCS's choice of notation (though she tended to use her own, such as the *x* notehead for indefinite pitch, where Herzog used a parenthetical normal notehead). RCS thanks Herzog in the "Music Preface" for checking the transcriptions of and making notational suggestions for *Callahan* and *Pauline*. These must certainly have been two of the most difficult transcriptions: *Callahan* is an extremely complex fiddle tune, and *Pauline,* a highly ornamented vocal blues (see below for more on *Pauline*).

vii. This section is sketched out in parts of LC47, but not in α. It was, apparently, later put back in β and β-m.

viii. The graphs and musical examples in this section are derived, successively, from one color plate (Figure 29A) in the section on this song in Milton Metfessel, *Phonophotography in Folk Music* (Chapel Hill: University of North Carolina Press, 1928), 81–86. RCS's graphs are drawn by hand, and are extractions and simplifications of the originals (to illustrate her ideas about the possibilities of scientific transcription). RCS was probably introduced to Metfessel's work by Charles Seeger, who had a lifelong interest in the melograph and this form of analysis—see his own writing about some of the same Metfessel material in "Prescriptive and Descriptive Music Writing," *Musical Quarterly* 44, no. 2 (April 1958): 184–95.

ix. Figure 1 is a redrawing by RCS of Fig. 29A (Graph 1) in Metfessel's book, though Metfessel's graph contains additional information. For an interesting discussion of this notational idea, and a good example of the historical lineage of RCS's unpublished ideas, see Jan Philip Schinhan, ed., "Even the Name Is New: Is It *folk-song* or *folk song* or *folksong*," *The Music of the Ballads,* The Frank C. Brown Collection of North Carolina Folklore, 4 (Durham, N.C.: Duke University Press, 1957), xxvii n. 23.

x. Figure 4, the line graph showing the durations, is not in the notes for these figures in LC47 (where Figure 4 is the complex musical notation example discussed below). It must have been added later in β-m.

xi. Figure 5, the music notation transcription from RCS's adapations of Metfessel's graphs, seemingly has two small errors in β-m. The first measure has a time signature of 14/16, but has fifteen 16ths in the music. The second measure has a time signature of 16/16, but has thirty-three 32nds in the music.

In LC47, there are two other versions of this same (complex) transcription. There is also a scratch page of arithmetic (probably in Charles Seeger's hand) for this figure, with beat counts sketched out. The first version of the figure (one single page labelled "Figure 4") is missing the dot on the third note of the first measure, and thus makes the measure 14/16. The second version of the example (on a page with five figures sketched in order, from the graphs to music notation, with actual 16th counts written under the music) has the dot. However, RCS's own "beat counts" have a slight error, counting three 16ths for the last two notes (the 16th and dotted eighth) rather than four. It is unclear what RCS eventually intended here, but this edition deletes the dot on the third note so that the notation agrees with the time signature.

The first version of the second measure in LC47 is notated differently from the one in β-m, but also contains too many beats (in fact, it is in 18/16). The second version in LC47 (with an accurate beat count below) shows clearly that the second-to-last note (a 16th note E in β-m) should be a 32nd note, which makes the measure 16/16, suggesting that it was simply miscopied into β-m.

In LC47 there are several pages of arithmetic calculations around these figures, as well as a complex chart labelled "Appendix on graphing and transcription techniques," which lists the timings for each word of this phrase of the song in each of her figures ("The syllables in Figures 1 to 5 are given the following transformations from Figure 1 to Figures 4 and 5"). This chart does not appear in α or β, and it did not seem useful to include it in this edition, as its primary function is to tabulate the scientific data underlying the figures. It is doubtful that RCS would have wanted it published except perhaps as an appendix.

xii. In the typescript there is a space left after the words "accented final" and an open and closed parenthesis, with a space between them, after the words "single tone." It could be that RCS meant to insert some symbol as explanation here, but it is unclear what it should be. It does not seem to be in the "Music Preface" to *OSC* nor in the transcriptions themselves.

xiii. In LC47 this unusual choice of words can be found, surviving into the later β:

The majority of those who read this book will, in all probability, be city or town people. They will be used to reading books, and may be able to read music notation more or less well. They must be warned, however, that *it is only to the extent to which they are, or become familiar with the idiomatic variations of American folk singing that they can expect to put approximately the right kind of flesh, blood and nerve fibre back on this skeleton notation.* (pp. 3–4, italicized words underlined in original)

The insights of these preceding paragraphs are equally pertinent to written scores in general—no doubt they are informed and nuanced by RCS the composer.

xiv. When RCS wrote this, none of the AFS recordings had been made available on record (the decision to do so was made in 1941). Since 1941, there have been many commercially available releases of these recordings. See the Editor's Introduction for a suggested list of resources.

xv. Compare, for example, Herzog on this same topic ("The Musical Notation Used in This Volume: An Explanation," in Lomax and Lomax, eds., *Negro Folk Songs As Sung by Lead Belly*):

> Our system of writing music, or for that matter any system, is at best but a kind of shorthand. As such it suggests, rather than reproduces, a musical idiom. In order to express another idiom, it must be modified. In any case, unless one has some acquaintance with the idiom it is difficult to interpret even the most adequate system. Sufficient acquaintance may even compensate for gross inadequacies. Those who are familiar with southern Negro singing would not require the sort of representation here attempted. But those unversed in it may find that the signs employed enable them to experiment and eventually get the swing. Even those who know the sound and feel of Negro rhythm may be interested in this effort to discover and analyse just wherein it is different from the sort for which our customary notation is adequate.

xvi. In α, at this point, RCS writes, "The second (B) has been chosen for use in the body of the book."

xvii. Pages 11 and 12 are not extant, and the material does not seem to appear in earlier typescripts. What seems to be missing, at least, is the example of three transcription styles for the song *Pauline*. So far, the example transcriptions (A, B, C) for *Pauline* have not been located. (See also Gaume, 244: "Rough typescript of a long introduction for *Our Singing Country*, approx. 60 pages. Lacks about a dozen music examples.")

The transcriptions of *Pauline* were intended as Figure 7. There are some handwritten pages about *Pauline* in LC47, but not the specific examples. It appears that in the earliest notes for this monograph, in one of the LC47 partial drafts called "A Few Remarks on Transcription," plans were made for these figures (with *Pauline* specifically singled out). However, it is likely that RCS never actually made this example. The following examples in her text illustrate the same point (variation, simplification).

Even assuming that these examples were never made (in final form), there is a natural segue that, perhaps, makes the transcription(s) of *Pauline*, which appears in tremendous detail in *OSC*, unnecessary here. It is possible that from RCS's viewpoint, there is nothing missing here (since the text flows evenly to the next set of examples). In β-m, a page is inserted at this point, with pencil indications made by an earlier researcher: "11 and 12 missing—are these pages necessary? [Name] 10–7–74." Underneath that is "missing 8/8/63" which appears to be in the same hand. Both these indications seem to point to the fact that pp. 11–12 from β are, at best, no longer extant, and, possibly, not intended to be there at all.

There are two transcriptions of *Pauline* in the "1001 Folksongs" Papers, one (A) marked "Moderately Slow" and one (B) marked "Slow" (without the tempo indication from *OSC*). (B) is cleaner, and slightly simpler than (A), which is itself simpler than the one in *OSC*. So, in effect, three successively more complex transcriptions of the tune *do* exist. (A) is quite marked up, (B) quite clean and in large part evidences the corrections in (A), so it is likely that (A) was a draft for (B). Both are reproduced below:

Figure E1

Figure E2

RCS clearly thought, from the attention she pays to it in this monograph, that Prothero's *Pauline* (AFS 176 B1, on Rounder 1823 and AFS L52) was a kind of "wonder among wonders" in this collection. (Allen Prothero was a singer from the Tennessee Penitentiary in Nashville who was recorded by Lomax [see *OSC*, Preface, xiv].) On the same recording session (AFS 176) is Prothero's solo performance of *Jumping Judy* (on AFS 12 and Rounder 1510, and probably the version RCS used in the "1001 Folksongs" Papers). In addition, AFS 177 (recorded at the same time) contains an extraordinary quartet version (with different lyrics) of *Pauline*, led by Prothero. Curiously, this quartet is almost certainly the same group as the one heard in *Dem Bones* (AFS 177 A2, again, led by Prothero, though he is not credited in *OSC*). Another version of *Pauline* can be found on AFS 232 B, by Albert Jackson, recorded in the state prison farm, Atmore, Alabama, by John L. Lomax in October, 1934. 232 B also includes an amazing quartet performance of *The Boston Burglar*, which is mentioned in LC47 and appears in the "1001 Folksongs" Papers (as *Boston Burgler*).

If AFS 176 is the recording of *Pauline* that RCS transcribed (and it almost certainly is), then, considering this song's importance, it is perhaps worth noting some subtle differences I hear between the transcription and the recording. For example, Prothero clearly says "Lawd it's trouble" rather than "well it's trouble" in the second page of the transcription (where RCS has "Well, it's oh, Lawdy me, well, it's trouble . . ."). In the very first measure, it would be reasonable to suggest an intermediate G (or at least an extra A!) between the F and the A on the first full measure. The voice doesn't fall (D? E flat?) in the 7th full measure at the end of the word "shanty." The first E flat in the transcription, is, to my ears is, at least, a neutral 7th.

Considering the tremendous fluidity of the performance (so striking to RCS), there *is* a kind of unapproachable limit of accuracy for a transcription like this. As RCS argues (and this song is strong evidence), western notation must inhabit a kind of middle ground between some kind of scientific, acoustic recording (which communicates little to someone wishing to recreate the performance) and a more useful, but highly detailed musical transcription. The "bridge must be neither too complex nor too simple."

xviii. "'Hollering songs' represent a distinct type of Negro folk singing. Usually they consist of a two-line stanza in which the singer repeats the first verse two or three times and the last verse once—the whole introduced and followed by long drawn-out moaning or 'yodling' or shouts in the tempo and mood of the tune he has been singing. They are sung with an open throat—shouted, howled, growled, or moaned in such a fashion that they will fill a stretch of the country and satisfy the wild and lonely and brooding spirit of the worker. The holler is a musical platform from which the singer can freely state his individual woes, satirize his enemies, and talk about his woman." (*OSC*, 348)

Marc Blitzstein, in his glowing review of *OSC* in *Modern Music* 19 (Jan.-Feb. 1942): 139–40, in which he "rates [*OSC*] with Bartók and Kodaly," was particularly interested in this song (the *OSC* title is *Make Me a Garment*; *Mamma, Mamma* is a previous song: but *Make Me a Garment* begins "Mamma, mamma, make me a garment"):

The one called *Mamma, Mamma, Make me a Garment* has the most astounding recitative quality, with a style of interval-leaping which sounds to a trained ear at first slightly amateurish or puzzling, but which on repetition yields a wild fresh juice. This is what we have all been talking about, when we said that the "folk art" must stimulate and fertilize the "fine art."

xix. *Belle* is on Rounder 1843.

xx. In the margin, in pencil, is written "worth" with the word "interesting" circled.

xxi. There is no Figure 14 included in the typescript, but it is likely that RCS intended to use the transcription of *John Riley* that appears in *OSC*, which is used in this edition. For *Oh Lovely Appearance of Death*, there is a one page example in β-m in RCS's hand, identical to that in *OSC* (except that it is in a mode of F rather than a mode of G as in *OSC*). This is the one used in this edition. It is hard to tell whether or not RCS meant there to be examples of transcriptions of different complexity (as in the previous figures) for these two songs.

In the *OSC* transcription for *John Riley,* RCS includes a meter change, extremely careful use of slurs and ties, and a number of other indications of the rhythmic freedom heard in this song. As such, it is possible that the example she intended here was of an even greater degree of notational complexity. AFS 1504 B, sung by Lucy Garrison, is quite free, both rhythmically (of which the published transcription gives some indication) and intonationally (in its widely varying and beautiful use of flat and neutral 7ths and 3rds).

RCS also mentions *John Riley* in α, in a section on the "model tune" that is presumed to be superceded by β (Section 11), in a footnote to the sentence:

b. The model tune should, however, with as few exceptions as possible, be that which is shown by majority usage to be most typical of the song as a whole.

The footnote (after the words "as possible") reads: "Two such exceptions will be found in measure 9 of *John Riley* and measure 3 of *Lowdown Lonesome Low.*"

xxii. Nye's performance, full of metrical variation so accurately transcribed in *OSC*, is on AFS L51 (*The Ballad Hunter*). The song and this performance are also discussed at length in John A. Lomax, *Adventures of a Ballad Hunter* (New York: Macmillan, 1947), 242–44, where it is called *The Dark-Eyed Canaler.*

xxiii. Jackson is still widely regarded as an authority on the shape-note and Sacred Harp repertory, and that of white spirituals. While acknowledged as a pioneer, his controversial attacks on claims of African American contributions to the spiritual were based on printed sources. His approach to sources primarily through print is contradicted by RCS's concern with the consideration of actual performance. Jackson worked closely with RCS after *OSC* (see Appendix 3).

xxiv. For information on Allen Prothero, see endnote xvii.

xxv. Figure 7 is missing from the sources; see endnote xvii.

xvi. In β, before the word "Sections," in footnote 6, the word "further" is written in pencil. In the typescript, no section numbers are given for this footnote reference, but it is likely that RCS is referring to Sections 10–12.

xxvii. Had this monograph been published earlier, RCS might have a clearer position in the intellectual history of formal ideas like interstanzaic variation and the "model tune" in the context of folk song transcription. Her discussion in this monograph predates much of the discussion of these ideas in American folk music literature. This is notable because since this monograph was not published, she has been egregiously overlooked in the standard history of American folk song scholarship. She was one of the first American folk song scholars/transcribers to deal seriously with a significant and consistent body of recorded folk music. It is likely that her writings, particularly on this topic (but others as well) would have become an integral and influential source for later scholars. See for example, the excellent article by Judith McCulloh entitled "What is the Tune?" in *Discourse in Ethnomusicology: Essays in Honor of George List,* ed. Caroline Card (Bloomington: Indiana University Ethnomusicology Publications Group, 1978), written almost forty years later, in which the author tries to determine methods for "abstracting the tune" and "settling on the basic tune," and states:

> But what if we find more than one stanza, printed, or if we hear or have a recording of a song that runs more than one stanza? We have several options, and the one we choose should depend on the nature of the song and on what it is we wish to compare. We can arbitrarily use the first stanza as our unit of musical comparison; we can choose one particular stanza that seems to be most representative; we can devise an archetypal stanza abstracted from transcriptions of all the stanzas in the performance; we can devise such a composite stanza more impressionistically, from simply listening to the whole performance.

and, a few paragraphs later:

> We might try to abstract a basic stanza, one that is ideally both adequate and uncluttered, from all the statements of a melody in any one performance. For instance, noncadential rests can be regarded as notes of equivalent length at the same pitch as the preceding note; repeated pitches within the same measure can be considered to be a single sustained pitch of equal total duration; pitches that occur at the same point in half or more of the stanzas ("majority usage") can then be used in the tune's abstract. . . .

Tick, in "Ruth Crawford, Charles Seeger, and 'The Music of American Folk Songs' " in *Understanding Charles Seeger, Pioneer in American Musicology,* ed. Bell Yung and Helen Rees (Urbana: University of Illinois Press, 1999), 117, also discusses the idea of "majority usage":

> Later he [Charles Seeger] adopted her term "majority usage," replying to a question about its provenance as follows: "I must admit that the term 'majority usage' was, to best of my knowledge, an invention of my wife Ruth's when she was working on the transcriptions of *Our Singing Country,* but maybe Cecil Sharp or even Percy Grainger used it.

See also George List, "An Approach to the Indexing of Ballad Tunes," *Folklore and Folk Music Archivist* 6 (Spring 1963): 7–16.

    xxviii. This sentence is heavily marked up in pencil in β, and these indications are incorporated into this edition.

    xxix. No Figure 17 is found in the typescripts, and RCS's reference to this song is unclear. Depending on how measures are counted in the published transcription of *As I Went Out for a Ramble* in *OSC*, measure 16 is either one note (the final word) or, more likely, a simple cadential turn with a different number of syllables each time (requiring slightly different melismas in different stanzas). However, that would be measure 14 or 15 (depending on whether the pickup was counted as a measure). It could be that RCS intended this as the simplest possible example of "majority usage," since a singer/reader could easily fit the different words to the melody in this measure.

xxx. The word "seen" is written above the word "felt" in pencil. Later in the sentence, the word "the" is written above "a" before "model tune." There is an additional, unreadable pencil phrase written after the end of the sentence.

xxxi. Although RCS frequently uses the term "fine-art" music in this monograph, this is the only time it is modified to be "occidental," though that word is used often in earlier manuscript sources (like LC47). Charles Seeger often used it in his writings.

xxxii. The words "of more complex songs" are not even a guess at the illegible pencil insert at this point, they are at best a paraphrase for the purpose of this edition. The pencil insert seems to be "of songs in more complex [?]." Since the final word is unreadable (and does not appear to be "singing styles"), the sentence is reconstructed to retain its intention, if not its actual wording.

xxxiii. *Job, Round the Bay of Mexico,* and *Dig My Grave* are on Rounder 1822, the latter two on AFS L5. There is a simplified transcription of *Dig My Grave* in the "1001 Folksongs" Papers. *Look Down That Lonesome Road* is on AFS 12 and Rounder 1510 (although Reed Prison Farm [*OSC*] is spelled "Reid" on AFS 12). *God Don't Like It (No, No)* is on AFS L52 (sung by D. W. White, who is not mentioned in *OSC*, which names just the choir).

xxxiv. In LC47, on the back of page 5 of an early manuscript, in pencil, there is a related, early version of these ideas: "In these cases, therefore, some one stanza—usually, but not necessarily, the first—has been selected as the 'model.'"

xxxv. *Georgia Land* is on Rounder 1827.

The Buffalo Skinners does not appear in *OSC*, and it is hard to know which recording of the tune RCS is referring to here. There are three entries in AFS with that title. Two are sung by John Lomax (2075 A, 10 inch LP, and 2088 B1, 8 inch LP). These are made three years apart (1936 and 1939); one was recorded by Charles Seeger. Another Lomax recording is available on AFS L28 and Rounder 1512.

The third (AFS 78 A4) is sung by Pete Harris, with guitar, Richmond, Texas, recorded by John A. and Alan Lomax, May 1934. This version, which is probably the one RCS is referring to, is on Rounder 1821 (under the name *Ranging Buffalo*). A note on the AFS catalog card says: "F.I 'I

Came out to Texas in 1845.'" But the version of *I Came to This Country in 1865* in *OSC* is sung by Jimmie Norris, Hazard, Kentucky, recorded by Alan and Elizabeth Lomax, Oct., 1937. There is a second version of *I Came to This Country in 1865* (AFS 1521 B2) and a song entitled *I Came to This Country, 1849* (AFS 1506 B2). *Buffalo Skinners* appears in the John Lomax and Alan Lomax, *American Ballads and Folk Songs* (New York: Macmillan, 1934).

On the other hand, the reference to *The Buffalo Skinners* in RCS's footnote may not pertain to a particular recording or its eventual possibility for inclusion in *OSC*. She may simply have been referring to a well-known song, or one she had heard Lomax sing.

xxxvi. *Long Summer Day* is mentioned only once in this edition and is on Rounder 1821, sung by the famous Clear Rock. There are a few instances in the various recordings and listings of these songs in which one or the other of either "Clear Rock" or "Iron Head" seems to be omitted in the documentation of a recording or transcription. A number of songs by these two singers are now available on the Rounder Library of Congress CDs (including a variant version of *Go Down, Ol' Hannah*, AFS 195 A2, on Rounder 1517 and 1826, AFS L8). For more on Iron Head and Clear Rock see Jerrold Hirsch, "Modernity, Nostalgia, and Southern Folklore Studies: The Case of John Lomax," *Journal of American Folklore* 105, no. 415 (Spring, 1992): 183–207, and chapter 7 of John Lomax, *Adventures of a Ballad Hunter*, entitled "Iron Head and Clear Rock." In *Adventures of a Ballad Hunter*, Lomax also discusses many of the other singers transcribed by RCS in *OSC*, including Allen Prothero, Roscoe McLean, Captain Nye, Vera Hall, and Doc Reed.

xxxvii. The relationship of the "fine-art composer" to the "ordinary" in the selection process for the tunes included in *OSC* is discussed by Cardullo (in "Ruth Crawford Seeger") and also, at some length by RCS herself in the eventual "Music Preface" to *OSC*, where she describes her own roles:

> But appreciation of the "nice and common" took root and grew strong, with promise of growing stronger as time goes on. And along with this growth have come surer answers to some of those questions of three years ago. *Careless Love* and *Adieu to the Stone Walls* are not sentimental, banal—that is, not if they are sung more or less in the manner in which the folk musician sings them.

For another, contemporary perspective on the relationship of the folk song scholar to the music, see Arthur Kyle Davis, Jr., "Some Recent Trends in the Field of Folksong," *Southern Folklore Quarterly* 1, no. 2 (June, 1937): 19–23. One of Davis's more interesting points vis-à-vis this monograph is that:

> it is undoubtedly true that among the newer converts to the cause of folk song are many musicians. Now this is a good sign and is as it should

be. Folk song is an amphibian form. Long enough has the purely textual study of folk song engaged the academic mind. It is high time for the musician to contribute his emphasis upon the tunes.

Note that, with respect to this edition, the title of Davis's article uses the single word "folksong," but the two words "folk song" are used in the body of the article. The same juxtaposition of the two variant usages occurs frequently in other articles from this period by Herzog and others.

xxxviii. In fact, RCS and her children were a large part of what made that "boom" occur. Her prescient statement makes it fascinating to imagine what she would have thought of the varieties of musical idea that constituted the folk revivals of the 1950s and 1960s.

xxxix. In this regard, Cardullo (in "Ruth Crawford Seeger"), Tick (in *Ruth Crawford Seeger*), and others have discussed the actual decision-making process for inclusion in OSC. Cardullo quotes Bess Lomax Hawes (27–28):

[RCS] felt that a lot of it simply couldn't be successfully transcribed for reproduction via books. There were pretty brisk arguments between all the people involved, because everybody had their own value system. Charlie sat in a lot of these sessions. I remember Ruth's concern that we weren't putting in enough ordinary material because everyone was so turned on by the extra-ordinary. That was a topic that was discussed a fair amount.

She exercised, mostly, a censoring capacity; that is, she would weigh it and say, "No, that really can't be done adequately in print, no matter how beautiful a song it is. There is no way to get it down so it would look right or be reproducible by someone who simply reads it." (Interview with Bess Lomax Hawes, August 1978)

xl. Tick, in her comparison of the writing of Charles Seeger and RCS's writing in this monograph ("Ruth Crawford, Charles Seeger, and 'The Music of American Folk Songs' "), cites this related passage in Charles Seeger's famous "Versions and Variants of 'Barbara Allen' in the Archive of American Folk Song at the Library of Congress," in *Selected Reports*, 1, 1 (Los Angeles: Institute of Ethnomusicology, University of California, 1966), 120–67:

It is difficult for urban Occidentals to recognize the fact that although variance may be the spice of life, invariance may be the meat. . . . The attitude, then, of the most admired traditional singer toward the song, tends to the serene and detached, however its end. Singing seems to be a natural thing for one to occupy himself with if he wishes. It requires of him no special preparation, effort, or pretense of an organized sort. . . . It is not a vehicle for pathos but seems to meet accepted requirements of ethos. In spite of the often romantic words, an almost classic reserve is maintained.

xli. This fascinating paragraph, discussing folk music's lack of "drama," or "artifice," also characterizes the compositional aesthetic that RCS helped to develop. See, for example, her *Piano Study in Mixed Accents* (which "just stops" when its formal trajectory is complete), or the 4th Movement of her *String Quartet*. Both of these well-known works foreshadow trends in twentieth-century "fine-art" music more or less accurately described by this paragraph about American folk song performance. By comparison, the composer Christian Wolff, in characterizing his own music and that of the so-called 1950s "New York School" (Cage, Feldman, Brown, Wolff), uses the term "musical rhetoric" (and talks about avoiding it).

In the "Music Preface" to *OSC*, she is succinct: "*Do not sing 'with expression,' or make an effort to dramatize.*"

See also Stith Thompson, ed., *Four Symposia on Folklore* (Bloomington: Indiana University Press, 1953), 193, quoting RCS (also quoted in full in Cardullo, 26):

> Here were things that weren't just beautiful melodies—a sort of unfinishedness in the music, it kept on going. Professional music isn't like that, it always tells you when it's going to end. Vigor is an overused word, but it certainly is there—non-stop, rhythmic quality, and chiefly, the thing I was talking about a while ago, improvisational qualities. If only you could play with this music, if you could bring it right home.

Also see the articles "Pre-School Children and American Folk Music" and "Keep the Song Going!" included in this edition for more on RCS's use of these ideas in teaching children.

xlii. In LC47, 9, RCS notes that *Dig My Grave* begins at $\quarternote$ = 64, and ends at $\quarternote$ = 104.

xliii. Figure 21 is not referred to by number in the typescript.

xliv. *Pay Day at Coal Creek* is on AFS L2. In α, this song is called "The Mines at Coal Creek," with the words "The Mines" crossed out and "Pay Day" written above, with a pencil indication: "Editor: please check the name of this song." In β, it is called *Pay Day on Coal Creek*.

This is one of the most famous, unusual, and influential recordings in the AFS collection (because of Pete Steele's banjo playing and the extraordinary vocal phrasing). It is fascinating to see how even a song like this, which has become a part of the "canon" of American folk music, was, at the time RCS worked on these transcriptions, still unfamiliar enough to have an uncertain title. Another famous banjo performance by Steele, *Coal Creek March*, is on the Rounder *Treasury*.

xlv. A multi-metric transcription of *The Crooked Gun* appears in RCS's notes, and is reproduced below. In *OSC*, this is notated with variable length fermatas.

Figure E3

This figure relates to the ideas in Section 21 and also Section 17, where this song is discussed at some length.

xlvi. These songs are all included in OSC, which is what RCS means as the eventual "end of this volume."

xlvii. This section number is in the typescripts, and refers to the section on "Rest" in both the typescripts and this edition. This might be a mistake or a result of changing section numbers, and it is possible that Section 21c is the one referred to.

xlviii. There is an unreadable pencil phrase in β next to this figure, something like "start with [?] song itself [?] strong." In Charles Seeger's *Check-List,* this song is called *If I Get My Ticket, Lord.* The OSC version is on AFS L52.

According to her notes, RCS considered this song (but did not use it) in *Let's Build a Railroad,* but in a different version (called *If I Got My Ticket* in Charles Seeger's *Check-List,* AFS 3007 A1, sung by the Shipp family of Byhalia, Mississippi, recorded by Herbert Halpert in 1939. These singers have become well known for their recording of *Sea Lion Woman* on Rounder *Treasury.* Interestingly, RCS's notes (October 11, 1950, from "1001 Folksongs" papers) show that she considered a version of *Jumping Judy* (not Prothero's, but AFS 174 A2 sung by a Memphis work gang, recorded in 1933), and the Augustus Haggerty (et. al) version of *Hammer Ring* (AFS 213 B2 recorded by John and Alan Lomax at the state penitentiary, Huntsville, Texas, in 1934, not AFS 219 A2 or 184 B2, the versions on Rounder 1826), which she *did* use.

xlix. In the "1001 Folksongs" Papers: *Lolly Trudum.* Other spellings/versions of this song available to RCS were *Rolly-Too-Rum* (AFS 1572 A1), and *Rolly Trudum* (AFS 2838 B1 and AFS 3016). Another version is available on AFS L12, *Anglo-American Songs and Ballads* (edited by Duncan Emrich).

l. These values are not in β, but from α and the "Music Preface" to OSC.

li. This reference to footnote 27 as well as the reference in footnote 19 to the same place, are ultimately referring to Figure 42, not extant. Figure 42 was probably intended as a chart showing metrical similarities of eight of the Negro work songs from OSC (all from Section 6 of OSC, entitled "Negro Gang Songs"). It has not yet been located, and may never have been made.

lii. In β, the word "The" follows the period, but no sentence follows. In α the following appears: "There are few exceptions to this practice (see *Take This Hammer*)."

liii. In the typescript, Figure 26 is missing (b), but the name of the tune is supplied. Although much of this tune exhibits the kind of off-beat singing RCS discusses here, only the first three measures are used in this edition as an example, taken from *OSC*.

liv. *Mamma, Mamma* ("Mama, Mama") is on Rounder 1826.

lv. The reference to Guido Adler in footnote 23 is without specific citation in the typescript. It is unclear to which of Adler's writings RCS intended to refer. Adler was an early-music and Wagner scholar who wrote mostly in German. He wrote a number of more general articles for the *Musical Quarterly,* in English, in the 1920s and 1930s which RCS could have been familiar with ("Internationalism in Music," 11 [1925], and "Style Criticism," 20 [1934]), but do not appear to be relevant to the subject at hand.

lvi. *Billy Barlow,* along with *John Done Saw That Number, The Wind Blow East,* and a few others, are songs from *OSC* mentioned in this typescript and later included in *American Folk Songs for Children.* Other songs were included in two other children's books: *American Folk Songs for Christmas* and *Animal Folk Songs for Children.*

lvii. *King William Was King George's Son* is available on New World Records, Recorded Anthology of American Music, *Oh My Little Darling, Folk Song Types,* NW 245 LP.

lviii. The word "Illustration" is written in pencil above the word "Comparison."

lix. See endnote l regarding Figure 42.

lx. The phrase "work song section of this" is pencilled in, very lightly, probably in RCS's hand, between "in this" and "collection of transcriptions."

lxi. There is an apparent inconsistency in the references to *Godamighty Drag.* In footnote 1, RCS mentions that this song was "dictated to the transcriber by the singer." In footnote 29 she says it was "heard in Texas." This is cleared up by *OSC*: "From the singing of Alan Lomax, learned from the singing of Augustus Haggerty, and a group of Negroes, Huntsville Penitentiary, Texas, 1934." This song is AFS 182 B2, and Bruce Jackson's liner notes for it on Rounder 1826 also point out the unusual transmission of this song. (Note, curiously, that the lyrics in *OSC*, "We went to see the Brazis" are not on Rounder 1826, *Big Brazos.*)

lxii. The words "Examples" is written in pencil above the word "Mention."

lxiii. Although there are four other songs mentioned in this edition which were not included in *OSC, Drop 'em Down* is the only one of these specifically cited by RCS as not included. This text is from β, and the other three tunes (they are, excepting *The Buffalo Skinners: Washington the Great, Au Long de ce Rivage,* and *The Raving Shanty Boy*) are mentioned only in α. Even more curious is her use, in the footnote, of the title *This Singing Coun-*

try, indicating that the title changed at some point after this part of the monograph was written. A transcription called *Drop 'em Down* is included in the Lomax Family Papers (see Appendix 2). The title *This Singing Country* is also used in earlier manuscript versions of the Lomax introduction to the book (in the Lomax Family Papers).

According to Charles Seeger's *Check-List,* there are at least three versions of *Drop 'em Down* in the Archive of Folk Song:

1) AFS 208 B2, sung by the famous "Mose (Clear Rock) Platt and group of Negro convicts," at the Central State Farm, Sugarland, Tex., recorded by John A. and Alan Lomax, 1934 (although on the original recording the equally famous Iron Head, James Baker, is credited as well)

2) APF 214 A1, "sung by a group of Negro convicts with ax-cutting," State penitentiary, Huntsville, Tex., recorded by John A. and Alan Lomax, 1934 (this is the same group that sings, for example, *Pick a Bale of Cotton* on Rounder 1821)

3) AFS 241 A2, "sung by a group of Negro convicts," Tucker State Farm, Tucker, Ark., recorded by John A. Lomax, 1934.

Neither 214 A1 or 208 B2 seem to be in 5/4 on the recordng, but are antiphonal 4/4 songs throughout. There is a transcription of 208 B2 in the "1001 Folksongs" Papers, which suggests that this is the version of the tune to which RCS refers. This transcription, which would be simpler because of its intended use, is in 2/4. The transcription of *Drop 'em Down* in the Lomax Family Papers is more complex, but only eight measures, and differs from that in the "1001 Folksongs" Papers and Figure 43 (above) in a number of ways (including tempo, which is ♩ = 76, and metrical grouping).

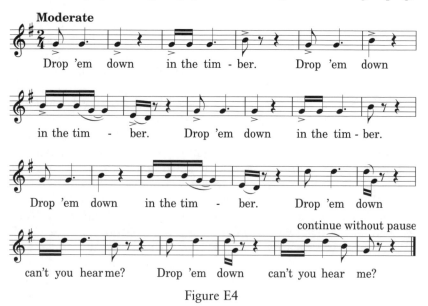

Figure E4

lxiv. In *OSC, Ain't Workin' Song* is notated in 9/8 with a shift to 8/8. The shift to 8/8 occurs only in the final stanza, which has an added line.

lxv. *Choose You a Seat 'n' Set Down* is on AFS L3, AFS L52 and Rounder 1510 (as *Choose Your Seat and Set Down*).

lxvi. The three figures and the text from the beginning of the words "or a continuous 2/8 as in *Roll On, Babe*" appear on a page whose order in β is unclear. This edition assumes that these three figures conclude Section 20, but there is no way to be certain (since, for example, RCS does not, for these three figures, specify what the "sung" meters are for these songs, only which meters have been used for the notation). The original meters in the second set of figures for this section (50–52) are assumed to be irregular or more complex than the simplified meters of these examples.

lxvii. The organization of Section 21 is confusing in the sources. The β Table of Contents is as follows:

21. Metrical irregularities—prolongation and contraction of measure
    a. Contraction of measure
    b. Prolongation of measure—the extended tone and the extended or inserted rest
    c. Underlimit of metrical irregularity shown in notation, especially with regard to extension of tone and extension and insertion of rest
    d. Manners of notating the extended tone and the extended or inserted rest.

There is no subsection called "Contraction of measure" in either α or β. Both typescripts suggest only three subsections, starting with 21.a "Prolongation of measure . . . ", with an untitled introductory section preceding that. The addition of 21.a ("Contraction") was probably inserted in the Table of Contents to plan β's redrafting, and then revised to exclude that subsection.

Much of Section 21 in β is scrambled, and required editorial reconstruction. Several pages in β and β-m, especially in this part of the typescript, are renumbered, out of order, numbered with "a" and "b," and so on. A few trail off, incomplete, but are begun again elsewhere, rewritten.

lxviii. Material from the word "song" to the end of Figure 55a is from a page in β-m. At the bottom of page "[53a]" in β, the paragraph "Prolongation and contraction of measure will be noted most frequently in these transcriptions at the breathing places in the . . ." begins, but does not continue elsewhere in β. This sentence (continued in β-m), along with its continuation "song—the singer either increasing or decreasing the moment between the end of one phrase and the beginning of another" is also found in α, with examples and a footnote. The footnote, attached to the phrase "An established norm of 2/4 may thus be felt to be momentarily . . . ," is as follows:

Although for ease in reading this has been notated as an extension of the preceding 2/4 measure, comparison with the parallel ending of phrase 1 indicates its nature as a contraction.

RCS cites *The Little Brown Bulls* as another example of prolongation to a 5/4, *Prison Moan* as a contraction of 4/4 to 3/4, *Santy Anno* as a prolongation of 4/4 to a 5/4, *Big Fat Woman* and *The Lady of Carlisle* as 4/4 to 6/4. She also notes: "Similar examples of prolongation and contraction of measure, within the phrase, will be found in *De Come Back Again, East Virginia, Fare Ye Well, My Darlin'* and many other songs."

There is an intermediary version of this passage in β-m, apparently rewritten from α and later revised (and consolidated in various ways) for β. In both β-m and α the earlier passage beginning with "It is a question, of course, whether the term 'departure' should be used . . ." is a footnote. In β-m the footnote quoted above (from α) is as follows, referring to *Po' Lazus*:

Although this 1/4 measure has been notated, for ease in reading, as an extension of the preceding 2/4 measure, its contractive character may be clearly discerned by comparison with the parallel ending of phrase 1.

The several extant rewrites of this subsection are illustrative examples of the process by which RCS wrote and edited this monograph.

lxix. At this point, in β-m, the words "of the phrase" are crossed out, probably by RCS, so they have not been included in this edition. The parenthetical sentence would have read "or, occasionally, section of the phrase."

lxx. The following five song examples (Figures 53–55) are taken from OSC. They do not exist in the typescript sources. They are not referred to in β. In β-m they are cited (without notation) as Figures 50–52 (*Po' Lazus/ Lolly Too-Dum, Johnny Stiles, Tee Roo/The Irish Lady*), on an insert page which seems to belong here in Section 21.a. It is likely that the insert page in the typescript with the other Figures 50–52 (see endnote lxvi on the figures for *Oh, Roll On, Babe, Little Bird . . . , Choose You a Seat . . .*) was made later in the revision process.

Lolly Too-Dum, in OSC, does not change meter, but uses a special fermata to indicate expansion. However, this song seems to have been an important metrical example to RCS even at the early stages of writing. In LC47, at this point, there is a yellow piece of paper clipped to another page of pencil indications, both clipped to page 9 (of an early typescript), with the note: "As a result a 2/4 becomes a 3/4 (e.g. Lolly Too Dum)."

For *Johnny Stiles,* the OSC transcription simply carries the footnoted phrase "Throughout all stanzas, half rests either are shortened by one beat or—more often—are omitted entirely," making it likely that RCS intended to put in some meter changes but simplified the notation further for OSC. The example in this edition is reconstructed to show a meter change where RCS probably intended. See the final sentence of Section 21.

In OSC, *Tee Roo* is notated in straight 3/4, without metrical or articulative time prolongations except for an apostrophe indicating an inserted rest. However, *The Irish Lady* contains prolongations to both 4/4 and 5/4, notated by alternative fermatas. Both examples are re-notated in this edition to include metrical changes illustrating RCS's point.

lxxi. There are faint, mostly unreadable pencil indications in this sentence, which might make the sentence: "An established norm of 3/4 may be felt to be momentarily contracted to 2/4." In parentheses "a 1/4 or a" is crossed out, probably by RCS, before "2/4."

lxxii. In β there is an unreadable pencil annotation here. In α RCS also writes:

> Similar examples of prolongation and contraction of measure, within the phrase, will be found in *Do Come Back Again, East Virginia, Fare Ye Well, My Darlin'*, and other songs.

What is problematic, for the purposes of this edition, is that the one-paragraph/one-example passage here in β beginning with "Prolongation or contraction of an established measure-length . . ." and ending with Figure 56 (*I Came to This Country . . .*) has an alternate, seemingly intermediary version in β-m. This three-page passage includes four notated examples (*Lolly Too Dum, I Came to This Country, East Virginia,* and *Texas Rangers*), and discusses "balance shown in inter-phrase occurrence of . . . prolongation." These figures are numbered in a confusing manner, as 60, 63/64 (both for *I Came . . .*), 65, and 66. They are identical to the *OSC* transcriptions except that they use meter changes rather than fermatas and apostrophes to indicate prolongations (as is done in this edition in several reconstructed examples).

These three pages were probably an intermediary step between α and β, but were deemed too long and detailed for the rewrite to β. They are not included in this edition; the four figures are represented by only one (Figure 56).

lxxiii. Figure 56 is missing from β, but is in the three-page insert from β-m referred to above. In addition, there is a two-page insert in β-m which consists of a page of unreadable pencil notes which seem to refer to "Contraction within the limits of a phrase" and the song *The Bachelor's Lay*. This song exists in full transcription in β-m, exactly as it appears in *OSC* except that all E flats in the *OSC* transcription are E naturals in the handwritten transcription.

lxxiv. Throughout the typescript, RCS uses "Bahaman" instead of the more modern "Bahamian." "Bahaman" is used in *OSC*.

lxxv. In β, the text ends in the middle of the word "promiscuity." This section continues a few pages later (pagination in the typescript is confused here). The word "promiscuity" is clear in an α footnote, which is integrated into the body of the β's text.

lxxvi. Figures 57–61 are missing from β; they are reconstructed from *OSC*. They illustrate fixed length fermatas and multiple commas. A full explanation of these is in the "Music Preface" to *OSC,* whose examples and symbols are used for this edition.

lxxvii. In the "1001 Folksongs" Papers, RCS used a different version of this tune, AFS 5266 A, sung by Vance Randolph and Sula Hudson, Crane, Missouri, 1941.

lxxviii. The fermata symbols with 4 and 5 above them are missing from the typescript but taken from the "Music Preface."

lxxix. The double comma is missing from the typescript, but taken from the "Music Preface."

lxxx. This figure is missing from the typescript, but taken from *OSC*. There is also a simplified transcription of *Ox Driving Song* in the "1001 Folksongs" Papers.

lxxxi. On AFS L12, AFS L52, Rounder 1510, and Rounder *Treasury*. Of interest is this song's similarity to *Don't You Hear the Lambs a' Crying?* (AFS 917 A2, sung by Melinda Jones, Austin, Texas, recorded by John A. Lomax, 1937), which appeared as RCS's moving piano arrangement in *American Folksongs for Christmas*.

lxxxii. *Soon one Mornin', Death Come Creepin'* is on AFS L53. In α, *My Father Gave Me a Lump of Gold* is included in this list.

lxxxiii. In LC47 (p. 12), the language is slightly different for this explanation of reducing triplets and quintuplets to duple approximations. RCS says that these subdivisions consitute "particularly elusive types of rubato," and that "triplets are still looked at askance by some musicians." She says "both of these types of rubato are well known in jazz and swing practice. . . ."

lxxxiv. There is a footnote number attached to the text in β at this point, with no corresponding footnote. In α, however, there is some additional text following "those omitted," which, for this edition, is assumed to be the intended footnote text.

In α, following the song title *Pauline,* is the phrase: "which, in this version, is closely allied to the holler through its style of performance." The same phrase also occurs in β, in the final paragraph of Section 9, in the discussion of "simplicity," and is in that section for this edition.

lxxxv. This section occurs much earlier in α, directly preceding the section entitled "Metrical irregularities—prolongation and contraction of measure" (now Section 21).

lxxxvi. In α: "Rests are an integral part of the artistry of singing." β's text for this section is considerably longer than α's.

Blitzstein, in his review of *OSC* in *Modern Music*, cites RCS's attention to rests:

> And Mrs. Seeger, who has done the editing, hears with extraordinary precision and love. In particular, she hears a pause as a pause, not as a tied-over note or as an aimless wait until the next line; some of the rests, as in *God Don't Like It* are really thrilling in the way they evoke the singer's breathing apparatus and niceness of phrasing. Five-fours, six-eight-plus-three-fours, etc., hold no terrors for her; if it was sung like that, that's the way it gets notated, and no nonsense.

lxxxvii. Figure 63 is missing in the typescript and is taken from *OSC*.

lxxxviii. In the typescript the following incomplete parenthetical phrase appears: "(—as, for instance, in Figures ." but no designations appear in α or β. Some possible examples are *John Done Saw That Number, The Banks of the Arkansaw,* and *Little Bird, Go Through My Window.*

lxxxix. The comma follows an open parenthesis in the typescript and is a very deliberate, if unusual parenthetical commatic construction.

xc. Interestingly, the footnotes RCS mentions here appear in *OSC* as specific annotations of individual transcriptions. This fuller explanation of rest-notation, written for this monograph to help contextualize those footnotes, never appeared.

xci. Section 24a is from β.

xcii. Section 24b, "Number of phrases to the stanza" is mostly from β, but is incomplete in the typescript. At this point in the typescript RCS probably had to abandon work on the monograph in favor of completing the "Music Preface" for publication, under difficult deadlines. (See Tick, chapters 16 and 17.) The rewritten manuscript seems never to have been completed. Therefore, after Section 24b, α is used for the most part. (See Editor's Introduction, "Provenance.")

In β, Section 24b is entitled (in the body of the text): "Number of phrases to the stanza," but in the Table of Contents, "Number of phrases to the song" (as it is called in the text of α). The former ("stanza") is used in this edition for two reasons. First, it is a reasonable supposition that the body of the text is a more current revision than the Table of Contents page, which seems to have been constructed first for organizational purposes (and has no page numbers). Second, the first sentence of this section refers to the number of phrases "to the stanza," not to the song.

The distinction here between "stanza" and "song" may not be especially important—they are, for the purposes of the discussion in this section, functionally equivalent. The use of this title creates a slightly different Table of Contents for this edition than that of the manuscript source reprinted and referred to by Cardullo in "Ruth Crawford Seeger" and Tick in *Ruth Crawford Seeger* (taken directly from β).

The entire text for Section 24b in α is:

About two-thirds of the songs exhibit two or four phrases to the song; a sixth, three phrases; a scattered dozen, five phrases. The remainder are too diverse in type to admit of discussion here.

In addition, there is one final, incomplete sentence in β:

With respect to inner organization of the musical materials of the phrase, and comparison of the interrelation of tonal and rhythmic patterns shown,

which is where β ends precipitously, leaving 3/4 of the page blank.

xciii. On AFS L1, Rounder 1521, and Rounder *Treasury.*

xciv. *When de Whale Get Strike* is on Rounder 1822.

xcv. There is a quotation mark in the typescript at the beginning but not the end of the word "blues."

xcvi. β "ends" here, on its page 61, but has Table of Contents entries for the sections that follow. Except for the confusion in this section (noted above), the monograph appears to continue more or less seamlessly in (the earlier) α. It is possible (as discussed above) that RCS, knowing that the monograph was complete as a composite (between β and the end of α), stopped working on β when deadlines for publication of *OSC* became pressing (and it was clear that the entire monograph would not be published). The end of α is more complete and clearly written than the beginning, with fewer corrections than in preceding sections.

In the current edition α is the source from this point on. As noted in the Editor's Introduction, however, this edition mostly follows β's Table of Contents, even when that means reordering sections in α.

xcvii. This section, called "Interstanzaic variation," is not in β, but appears in α and β-m. In α there seems to be a diagonal line through the whole section, which might mean it was meant to be completely rewritten (since there is an "entry" for it in the table of contents of the later typescript). This is likely, since the section is recast for β-m. It is numbered as Section 12 in both α and β-m.

Another possibility (not followed in this edition) is that RCS intended to delete this short section (a few paragraphs), since she discusses "interstanzaic variation" in other places (see, for example, Section 8: "Majority usage") and from several distinct musical perspectives.

The first paragraph is not found in α, but in β-m. The second paragraph is similar in those two sources. The third paragraph is found complete only in α.

In this edition, this section (as well as Sections 27–30) is taken primarily from β-m, along with contributions only found in α. In the notes on this and remaining sections, many minor variations between the two sources are noted: it is possible that neither was a final version.

xcviii. "factor" in α.

xcix. "found" in α.

c. There is faint, illegible written text here after the word "evidence" which seems to be "even in the simplest singing style," changing the sentence to: "Even without (or with slight) change of stress in the word, of various stanzas, it is constantly in evidence, even in the simplest singing style (see, for instance, . . .)"

ci. A number of songs from this point on (including *The Raving Shanty Boy*) do not appear in *OSC*, and so no transcriptions are available for these examples. Since α and β-m were earlier versions, a number of songs RCS mentions here, which she may have transcribed, did not make the final edition of *OSC*.

cii. This song, AFS 2355 A, is not in *OSC*. It is sung by John Norman, Munising, Michigan, 1938, and was recorded by Alan Lomax. There is, in the "1001 Folksongs" Papers, a typescript of the lyrics and a very rough sketch of the transcription (first verse and first refrain), with the lines out of order and then correctly renumbered. The musical transcription is called "The Roving Shanty Boy," as it is referred to in α, while the lyrics in the "1001 Folksongs" Papers are correctly titled *The Raving Shanty Boy*. It is hard to know which measure RCS is referring to here by "measure 3," but it is probably the third complete measure ("love to sing and dance," "will spend my money free," "mud clear to the knee"). She makes the point, very clearly heard when listening to the recording, that the lyrics vary considerably over a simple rhythmic melodic figure, producing significant interstanzaic variation in a simple tune.

RCS's entire transcription is included in this edition (and put it in correct order). The complete lyrics are:

I am a raving shanty boy, love to sing and dance
I wonder what my girl would say if she could see my pants;
Fourteen patches on my knee, sixteen on my stern,
Wear them whilst out in the woods—homeward they return.
(Refrain):
Still I'm a jovial fellow, will spend my money free,
Take a drink most any time—lager beer with me.

You ought to see my Liza, she's my dark-eyed lassie,
And she thinks a pile of me,
You ought to see her throw herself when I get on a spree;
Trots off like some quarter horse, sailing round the horn,
With her head and tail up like a steer rushing through the corn.
(Refrain):
Still I'm a jovial fellow, will spend my money free,
Take a drink most any time—whiskey clear with me.

With my patched-up pants and river boots, mud clear to the knee,
Lice on me like cherry pits, wrastling with the fleas —
Still I'm a jovial fellow, will spend my money free,
Take a drink most any time—whiskey clear with me.

The recording is followed by an illuminating interview with Norman by John Lomax. Because this song was *not* included in *OSC*, a transcription of this interview is included below (sometimes Lomax or Norman's voice is unintelligible on the recording, indicated by [ ]):

John Norman: Why, I learned that in a little camp down in lower Michigan, way back in '98.

John Lomax: Do you remember who sang it?

JN: Jack Osberry

JL: Was he [ ]?

JN: Pretty fair, yes.

JL: Was this a popular song at the time?

JN: It was, yes, at that time.

JL: So you've sung it all over Michigan?

JN: Oh yes, I've sung it for years. For sure lately I don't know when I've sung it now till just tonight.

JL: And what's your full name?

JN: John Norman.

JL: And how old are you?

JN: 62

JL: And you were born in?

JN: Isabel County.

JL: That's where?

JN: In the farming country out from up Pleasanton you know.

JL: And what was your father?

JN: Joseph D. Norman.

JL: Was he a [ ] or a mulatto [ ] and your mother?

JN: She was mulatto too, black and brown, like a [ ].

JL: And they both [ ]?

JN: Oh yes, they come to Michigan in the early day, when they were young.

JL: And how many years did you stay in one place?

JN: Well I started to work in the lumberwoods, away from home. I worked for my father till I was around 12 or 13, but I left home out into the camps at the age of 15 and I practically been in them off and on ever since—odd times I was farming.

JL: What states did you work in?

JN: Michigan, Wisconsin, Minnesotee, Ideeho, Mountana, Washington and I was up in British Columbia.

JL: Most of the time in Michigan though?

JN: I put in more time in Michigan than any other place, yes.

Norman is also represented in the Archive by two other OSC songs, *The Little Brown Bulls* (AFS 2356 B, 2357 A1) and *The Wild Colonial Boy* (AFS 2359). RCS also includes another Michigan version of this tune in the "1001 Folksongs" Papers (*The Wild Colonial Boy*, from Evelyn Elizabeth Gardner and Geraldine Jencks Chickerings, *Ballads and Songs of Southern Michigan*, [Ann Arbor: University of Michigan Press, 1939]). Norman's is the version used in OSC. The recording includes a short interview with Lomax, which is condensed and rewritten into one complete narrative paragraph in OSC.

ciii. *Washington the Great*, AFS 1337 B1, is not in OSC, and is only mentioned once, in this short section of α. The song is sung by Mrs. Minta Morgan, Bells, Texas, recorded by John Lomax in 1937. A transcription of it is included in Duncan Emrich's *Folklore of the American Land* (Boston: Little, Brown and Co., 1972), 406–7. This transcription is probably of the same recording, which is available on *Songs and Ballads of American History and of the Assassination of Presidents* (Rounder 1509 and AFS L 29).

A transcription (by RCS?) is also included in the "1001 Folksongs" Papers, where it is notated in 3/8 as opposed to 6/8 in Emrich (otherwise, it is exactly the same). The song is also cited in John W. Beattie, *The American Singer: Book Five* (New York: American Book Co., 1950–52).

Figure E5

This song is listed in AFS as "Tape 98," which also includes AFS 1331 B thru 1336 B3 on Side A, AFS 1337 A1—1343 A5 on Side B. 1337–1338 are absent on the tape (Side B starts with *The Play Goes On till Morning*, sung by Minta Morgan). Missing songs are:

1337

    A1: *The Bachelor's Lay* (also referred to in this edition, and in OSC)

    A2: *The Banks of Arkansas*

    A3: *Washington the Great*

    B2: *The Close of the Day*

1338

    A1: *The Cowboy's Ride*

    A2: *When I Die I Want to go to Heaven*

    B1: *The Southern Soldier*

    B2: *Jennie, Get the Hoecake On*

At present, the actual disks are missing as well from the Library of Congress.

    civ. Figure 65 is not specified exactly in the typescript, and is probably an unlocated or intended transcription of variation in *Oh, Roll On, Babe*.

    cv. Section 26 is from α.

    cvi. *Les Clefs de la Prison* is on AFS L5 and Rounder 1842. This may be the song Bess Lomax Hawes refers to in her moving recollection of RCS at work on *OSC*, which also points to RCS's singular, intense focus on the intrinsic qualities of the music itself ("Reminiscences and Exhortations: Growing Up in American Folk Music," *Ethnomusicology* 39, no. 2 [Spring/Summer, 1995]: 179–94):

She taught me that professional, academically trained, avant garde, politically radical, totally up-to-the-minute musicians like Charles Seeger and Ruth Crawford Seeger could and did stand in awe of the musical achievments of old country ladies, black stevedores, Mexican field workers, Ohio canal boat captains, and all the other amazing casts of characters my father and brother had been for so long re-introducing to their own homeland audiences. I already sort of knew all this, of course, but it was Ruth who diagrammed out for me the musical qualities I had been hearing—how smoothly and inevitably a 5/4 meter worked in a Cajun ballad, how rhythmically complex an apparently routine Kentucky fiddle tune [*Bonyparte? Callahan? Glory in the Meetin' House?*] turned out to be, how a meltingly liquid Alabama field holler really defied standard music notation.

cvii. Section 27 is from α and β-m. It is numbered Section 14 in both. β-m starts at the subsection called "Release."

cviii. Allen's book, referred to in the footnote, has been reprinted: *Slave Songs of the United States: The Classic 1867 Anthology,* edited by William Francis Allen, Charles Pickard Ware, and Lucy McKim Garrison (New York: Dover, 1995). The introduction to this older work deals with issues that RCS dealt with in her own work. For example, in discussing notation:

The difficulty experienced in attaining absolute correctness is greater than might be supposed by those who have never tried the experiment, and we are far from claiming that we have made no mistakes. I have never felt quite sure of my notation without a fresh comparison with the singing, and have often found that I had made some errors. I feel confident, however, that there are no mistakes of importance. What may appear to some to be an incorrect rendering, is very likely to be a variation; for these variations are endless, and very entertaining and instructive. (page v)

cix. From footnote 33 to the end of this edition, numbers do not correspond to those of β, since this material is drawn primarily from α and β-m.

cx. There is a variant of this on Rounder 1824, recorded the same year.

cxi. *Au Long de ce Rivage* is not included in *OSC,* and no transcription has been located (see also the Editor's Introduction). This song is AFS 14 B, sung by Elida Hofpauir, New Iberia, La. (also the singer for *Les Clefs de la Prison*), recorded by John A. Lomax. It is a long, beautiful, a capella performance. Hofpauir's father, Julien, and sisters, Elita and Mary, can be heard on Rounder 1842 (along with *Les Clefs de la Prison*).

cxii. Following this paragraph, there is one short paragraph more to this sub-section, bracketed and with the word "cut" next to it:

Grace-notes have been used sparingly in these notations, since they tend to clutter up the page. It will be observed that their pitch is frequently of the tone which precedes them. The slide from the grace-note to the following tone is usually rapid, and to be sung *before* the beat.

cxiii. In α, this paragraph is as follows (variations shown in brackets): Manners of tone release are many. They include, among others, the half-sung, half-spoken drop of the voice so characteristic of Negro singing (see *Samson*) and the quick upward [slide] heard frequently among both White and Negro singers. The pitch of these final tones is sometimes definite enough to allow their inclusion in customary notation [(see the final 16th in measure 4 of *Soon One Mornin' Death Come Creepin'*)]. At other times they are indicated by the symbol ♩.

cxiv. Section 28 is from α and β-m.

This section on *Intonation* and the following section on *Scale* are combined into one section in LC47, called "Intonation and Scale" (beginning on page 12). It is very different from the later passage, though it also includes a reference to Yasser. In its discussion of the number of scale degrees in a song, it mentions that there are four tones in the song *Little Sally Water* (not mentioned elsewhere), five in *Long Lonesome Road*, and six in *God Don't Like It*.

There are 12 entries in Charles Seeger's *Check-List* for *Little Sally* [*Walker, Water, Waters*]. The only one called *Little Sally Water* is recorded by Herbert Halpert, so that is probably not the one referred to by RCS.

LC47 also contains the following paragraph:

Pentatonic tonal systems are known the world over. Some of them (notably in Indonesia) comprise five equal tones per octave. If certain folk practices in present-day America approximate this intonation, we may ask: are they approaching Indonesian practice, or, showing a certain amount of stability, approaching Occidental fine art practice? We cannot answer any of these questions. If we contemplate the third alternative—rapprochement with Occidental fine art practice—we have the added question on our hands: is that fine art practice itself showing stability or change in the direction of other tunings? (p. 16)

cxv. Charles Seeger edited the series in which Yasser's famous book was published, and both Charles and RCS held Yasser's ideas in great esteem. Other American composers felt similarly—Harry Partch was also interested in Yasser's work, though respectfully critical in his well-known consideration of *The Theory of Evolving Tonality* in his *Genesis of a Music* (Madison: University of Wisconsin Press, 1949).

cxvi. This sentence is heavily marked up in the typescript, and probably would have been edited further had RCS rewritten it for β. What she means is that stanzas will vary according to intonation: in the same song, some stanzas will be more major, some more minor, some approximating a midpoint. In addition, there is a footnote here with the marking "cut" next to it:

It is a question to what extent these varying pitch levels are effected by variation of melodic context, such as approach from below or above, syllabification—whether rapid or slow—and so on.

cxvii. Note RCS's use of the term "heterophony," and that she finds it so "striking." This musical term and idea has been used often to describe RCS's own music, specifically with respect to her use of (dissonant) counterpoint and the "heterophonic ideal." (See Mark Nelson, "In Pursuit of Charles Seeger's Heterophonic Ideal: Three Palindromic Works by Ruth Crawford," *Musical Quarterly* 72, no. 4 [1986]: 458–75.)

cxviii. In this edition, this paragraph is a composite of β-m and a footnote at this place in α (cited in a previous endnote).

cxix. Section 29 ("Scale and mode") is from α (Section 16); a copy is inserted in β-m.

cxx. In this edition, the section referred to is Section 3 (in α), entitled "The model tune." This section became Sections 10 and 11 in β (and in this edition). In β-m the parenthetical remark is "(as stated in MUSIC APPENDIX I)."

cxxi. "To be sure, sometimes a more careful editor will discover that a particular sharp or flat does not occur in the melody and put this sharp or flat in parentheses, probably in order to indicate that it really is not present, but that the reader might *feel* it in that key. (See *OSC, Jennie Jenkins* [p. 129], to cite but one.) Then comes the dilemma. If there is a tune which does not use the complete major scale, but does use the leading tone—F sharp for example—the editor puts the signature of F sharp in parentheses (*OSC, Where Have You Been, My Good Old Man?*)." (Schinhan, *North Carolina Folklore,* Editor's Introduction, xxiii.)

cxxii. This figure from *Low Down Lonesome Low* is not in the typescript, but is taken from *OSC.* In the footnote in α, there is the handwritten phrase "See Insert attached," which might refer to the transcription for this piece.

cxxiii. "notating a single song" in α.

cxxiv. In α the following is inserted:
Transcriber A, for instance, may find a pentatonic scale and a Dorian mode. Transcriber B, distinguishing an extra small tone or two, may find a seven-tone scale and a Mixo-lydian mode. Transcriber C, with the aid of acoustic measuring devices, may uncover an almost infinite number of tonal elements yielding classification as a Hindu raga.
These three sentences are enclosed in pencilled-in square brackets in α, and not in β-m.

cxxv. RCS is the "Music Editor." For more on RCS and the "Music Editor" title, see Porterfield, *Last Cavalier,* 416.

cxxvi. Kolinski, an important ethnomusicologist and world music theorist, was also a fascinating composer whose compositions, like RCS's later works, integrated his interests in ethnomusicology. His more scientific, modernist, and, in my opinion, forward-looking theoretical approach to folk music would have certainly been of interest to RCS in her search for formalist methods. Curiously, his important (later) article on "contour theory" (Mieczyslaw Kolinski,, "The General Direction of Melodic Movement," *Ethnomusicology* 9 [1965]: 240–64) makes significant use of Charles Seeger's "On the Moods of a Music Logic,"*Journal of the American Musicological Society* 13 (1960): 224–61.

cxxvii. Section 30 ("Accompaniment") is from α (Section 16); a copy is inserted in β-m.

cxxviii. Note the different number (197) from that stated in the "subtitle" of this monograph ("more than three hundred"). The appendix for OSC contains listings for 205 songs. See Tick, 255: "By September of that year [1938] she had completed about 300 transcriptions. . . ." RCS mentions the number 300 or approximately that several times in print. (See her "Letter to John Becker," in Gaume, 207: [T]here were "three hundred folk songs" and she "transcribed all of them.")

Cardullo writes on p. 28 of her "Ruth Crawford Seeger," however, that "90 were finally chosen," and later, in "Ruth Crawford Seeger, Preserving American Folk Music," *Heresies: A Feminist Publication on Art & Politics,* 10 (1990), writes: "Ruth transcribed over 300 tunes from the Lomaxes' field recordings, from which 90 were finally chosen for the book." This number is not supported by any other evidence, and appears to be an error.

There are probably, then, approximately 100 transcriptions still unpublished. Some of the songs mentioned in this edition are transcribed in much simpler form in the "1001 Folk Songs" Papers. A few of these (*Drop 'em Down, The Raving Shanty Boy, Washington the Great, Au Long de ce Rivage*) are referred to in this current edition. Early sections of α (superseded by β) as well as even earlier sources (from LC47) mention a number of other songs not included in *OSC*.

Porterfield, on p. 429 of *Last Cavalier* mentions that Lomax had asked "Mrs. Seeger" to "send him all the material that had been deleted so that he could review it for possible use in his memoirs." Appendix 2 catalogues 34 transcriptions in the Lomax Family Papers at the Center for American History, Austin, Texas. These and any other extant transcriptions would of course be a subject for future scholarship and publication.

cxxix. The word "5–" is missing from β, but she clearly means "5–string banjo."

cxxx. This is an interesting and astute observation. It is now common for folk and old-time musicians to make this point: that guitar players tend to play songs in major, banjo and fiddle players in minor (probably because of the historically more common practice of minor open tunings on fiddle and banjo). For instance, the transcription of *Pretty Polly* in *OSC* is in major, and there are numerous commercial recordings of this tune played by old time guitarists in major keys (including the one transcribed for *OSC*, by E. C. Ball). However, AFS 1702 (on AFS L1 and Rounder 1511) contains an excellent example of the same tune in minor, played on banjo by Pete Steele (of *Pay Day at Coal Creek* fame).

A personal anecdote: while editing this monograph and listening to the songs, I often played and sang them for my young daughter. One of our favorites became *Pretty Polly,* which, listening to E. C. Ball's recording, I began to play on guitar in D major. I happened to play this guitar version for a friend, the old-time fiddler and banjo player Bert Porter from Glover, Vermont. He picked up his fretless banjo and played it in minor (which was, in fact, how I used to play it!), commenting with a wry smile that guitar players "always play the minor tunes in major."

cxxxi. Commonly called the "drone" string, or the "high" string today.

cxxxii. There is a minor difference here between α and β-m, whose brevity belies its possibility for confusion. In α, the word "one" is crossed out, but it appears in β-m. Without going through all 205, or possibly 300 original recordings and carefully checking for the presence of mandolins, it seems possible that, in fact, RCS wanted to delete the word "one" to be less specific about this unique occurrence. But if this is true, it casts doubt upon the manuscript order. Since everything else points to β-m being later than α (for the most part), for this edition it is assumed that she simply put the word "one" back in.

cxxxiii. *Callahan,* called *The Last of Callahan,* is on AFS L2, the (alternate, in the key of A) recording used for *OSC.* The tempo for this version ($\quarternote$ = 160), which has caused considerable alarm (and awe) over the years to musicians who have tried to play this tune, is, if anything, a bit slow.

In α, this paragraph is quite marked up and rearranged. RCS recast it for the later edition (further evidence for the order of β-m). In α the first sentence is:

> Fiddles appear, on these recordings, as accompaniment to the voices, only in company with other instruments. In *Batson* they maintain an independent melodic line, the guitar supplying the chordal basis. The string-band accompaniment to *Long Lonesome Road* also contains a distinctive fiddle figuration. An example of fiddle virtuosity in solo playing may be heard in *Callahan,* whose two simultaneous melodic lines are maintained by the one player at breakneck speed.

At least one more fiddle tune, the remarkable *Glory in the Meetin' House* (AFS 1536 A2, performed by Luther Strong, Hazard, Kentucky, 1937; on AFS L2 and Rounder *Treasury*) was transcribed in part (and is in the Lomax Family papers: see Appendix 2; the transcription is in G minor, but the recording seems to be in E minor), but not completed.

Ironically, of the two fiddle tunes RCS so painstakingly and accurately transcribed for (the published version of) *OSC,* the one *not* discussed here, *Bonyparte['s Retreat],* transcribed from the performance of the great W. H. Stepp, has become one of the most famous American musical signatures (as used by Aaron Copland in "Hoedown" from *Rodeo*).

According to Howard Pollack, in *Aaron Copland: The Life and Work of an Uncommon Man* (New York: Holt, 1999), Copland worked directly from RCS's transcription in composing *Rodeo,* possibly without hearing the actual recording (as the reader can, on Rounder 1518 and Rounder *Treasury*). Bess Lomax Hawes remembers, however, that:

> When I was a teenager working at the Library of Congress, such eminent composers as Aaron Copland and Virgil Thomson came in looking for some interesting musical folk idioms but most urgently for solid and long-lasting melodies for use in their symphonic compositions. And I helped find the field recordings that they listened to and later put to extensive use. (Hawes, "Reminiscences and Exhortations")

See also Tick, 270–72.

cxxxiv. This is "stanzas" in α, with the plural "s" crossed out, further support that β-m is a revision of α.

cxxxv. The word "each," not present in α, is inserted above the line in β-m.

cxxxvi. There is an unreadable pencil indication in β-m above and between the words "stanza" and "tending."

cxxxvii. There is a very faint typewritten page after this, with some handwriting over it that is almost impossible to read, but the following phrase can be discerned: "a vol. could be written on the . . . ." This is where the typescripts end, appropriately, with the words "the song proceeds."

Appendix 1

Songs Referred to in
The Music of American Folk Song

Many songs mentioned in this edition are spelled slightly differently in *OSC*. This list may assist the reader in finding in *OSC* and other sources the songs discussed in this edition. In the endnotes I have often cited currently available CDs (and LPs) of recordings transcribed and mentioned.

The list below contains only those songs appearing in this final edition. Every song on this list, with the exception of five (*Au Long de ce Rivage, The Buffalo Skinners, Washington the Great, The Raving Shanty Boy, Drop 'em Down*) appears in *OSC*. There are other songs, some of which appeared in *OSC*, and some of which did not, which are mentioned in sections of α and LC47, but not incorporated into this edition.

Adam in the Garden Pinnin' Leaves
Adieu to the Stone Walls
Ain't It Hard to be a Right Black Nigger?
Ain't Workin' Song
As I Sat Down to Play Tin-can
   (*OSC:* As I Set . . .)
As I Went Out for a Ramble
Au Long de ce Rivage
   (not in *OSC*, only mentioned in α)

Batson
Belle
Biddy, Biddy

Big Fat Woman
Billy Barlow
Black Jack Davy
Blanche Comme la Neige
Blood Strained Banders
   (*OSC*: The Blood Strained Banders)
Blue Bottle
Bugger Burns

Callahan
Chilly Winds
Choose You a Seat 'n' Set Down
Cotton Eyed Joe

Daddy Shot a Bear
Darling Corey
Dem Bones
Devilish Mary
Diamond Joe
Didn' Ol' John Cross the Water on His Knees?
Dig My Grave
Do Come Back Again
Doney Gal
Don't Talk About It
Don't You Like It
Down, Down, Down
Drive It On
Drop 'em Down
   (not in *OSC*)
Duncan and Brady
Dupree

East Virginia
Fare Ye Well, My Darling
   (*OSC*: Fare Ye Well, My Darlin')
Frenchman's Ball
   (*OSC*: The Frenchman's Ball)

Georgia Land
Go Down, You Little Red Rising Sun

God Don't Like It
God Moves on the Water
God a Mighty Drag
  (OSC: Godamighty Drag)

Hard Times in the Country
Harvey Logan
Haul Away, My Rosy
High Barbaree
  (OSC: The High Barbaree)
Hog Rogues on the Harricane
Holy Ghost
Hush Li'l Baby

I Came to This Country in 1865
I Got to Roll
If I Got My Ticket, Can I Ride?
I'm a Stranger Here
I'm Worried Now But I Won't Be Worried Long
I've Been a Bad, Bad Girl
  (OSC: I Been . . .)

Job
John Done Saw That Number
John Henry
John Riley
John Was a-Writing
  (OSC: . . . Was a-Writin')
Johnnie Won't You Ramble?
  (OSC: Johnny . . .)
Johnny Stiles

Katey Dorey
  (OSC: Katy Dorey)
Keep Your Hands on That Plow
King William
  (OSC: King William Was King George's Son)

Ladies in the Dinin' Room
Les Clefs de la Prison

Lexington Murder
   (*OSC*: The Lexington Murder)
Lights in the Quarters, Burnin' Mighty Dim
Little Bird, Go Through My Window
Little Bonny
   (β: Little Bonny; α: Little Bonnie)
Little Willie's My Darling
Lolly Too Dum
   (*OSC*: Lolly Too-Dum)
Long Lonesome Road
Long Summer Day
Look Down That Lonesome Road
Lord, It's Almost Done
   (*OSC*: Lord It's All, Almost Done)
Low Down Chariot
Low Down Lonesome Low
   (*OSC*: The Low-down, Lonesome Low)

Make Me a Garment
Mamma, Mamma
Married Man Gonna Keep Your Secret
Marthy Had a Baby
My Father Gave Me a Lump of Gold
My Old True Love

O Lawd I Went Up on the Mountain
O Lovely Appearance of Death
   (*OSC*: Oh, Lovely Appearance of Death)
Ol' Hannah
   (*OSC*: Go Down, Ol' Hannah)
Old Bangham
Old King Cole
Old Shoes and Leggin's
Over Jordan
Ox Driving Song

Pass Around Your Bottle
Pauline
Pay Day at Coal Creek
Peter Gray

Po' Farmer
Po' Lazus
  (*OSC*: Po' Laz'us)
Pretty Polly
Prison Moan

Roll On, Babe
  (*OSC*: Oh, Roll On, Babe)
Round That Bay of Mexico
  (*OSC*: . . . the Bay . . .)
Roustabout Holler
Run Along, You Little Dogies

Samson
Soon One Morning, Death Come Creepin'
Sweet William

Take This Hammer
Tee Roo
The Bachelor's Lay
The Beaver Island Boys
The *Bigler*
The Blood-Strained Banders
The Buffalo Skinners
  (not in *OSC*)
The Coal Miner's Child
The Crooked Gun
The Darkeyed Canaller
  (*OSC*: Dark-Eyed Canaller)
The Greenland Whale Fishery
  (*OSC*: Greenland Whale Fishery)
The Irish Lady
The Lady Who Loved a Swine
The Little Brown Bulls
The Raving Shanty Boy
  (not in *OSC*, only mentioned in α, but also called The Roving
  Shanty Boy)
The Reek and the Rambling Blade
The Rich Old Lady
The Rising Sun Blues

The Romish Lady
The Rowan County Crew
The Sporting Cowboy
The Texas Rangers
  (*OSC*: Texas Rangers)
The Vance Song
The White House Blues
The Wild Colonial Boy
The Wind Blow East
Three Nights Drunk
Toll a Winker
  (*OSC*: Toll-a-Winker)
Tom Bolyn
Trench Blues
Trouble, Trouble

Washington the Great
  (not in *OSC*, only mentioned in α)
When the Whale Get Strike
  (*OSC*: When de Whale Get Strike, also α: The Whale Get
  Strike)
Where Have You Been, My Good Old Man?

You Kicked and Stomped and Beat Me
You Turn for Sugar an' Tea
  (also α: "and")

Appendix 2

List of Transcriptions in the Lomax Family Papers, Center for American History, University of Texas at Austin

The Lomax Family Papers in the Center for American History, University of Texas at Austin, contain a number of materials related to *OSC* and *The Music of American Folk Song*. These papers include several drafts of the Lomax introduction to *OSC*, a collection of early versions of the lyrics to many of the songs, and (at least) 34 unpublished drafts of transcriptions made by RCS which were probably intended for *OSC* but not used.

The items in the archives are entitled:

> *Our Singing Country*: manuscript and notes
> *Our Singing Country*: rejected material

The difference between the number of songs RCS is said to have transcribed ("about three hundred") and the number of songs in *OSC* (205) is greater than 34 (even adding the four or five mentioned in *The Music of American Folk Song*). Thus, there are still about 60 transcriptions unaccounted for.

The transcriptions listed below are all reasonably final drafts, with many hand markings, corrections, and addenda. For several, the sources still need to be located (a project beyond the scope of this edition). This appendix is provided not so much as an authoritative study of these recently located manuscript sources, but as a starting point for further scholarship.

Some of these songs do not have AFS numbers written on them in the Lomax Family Archives manuscripts. For many of them, in the list below, specific recording numbers have been reconstructed, and listed next to the song. Most are in Charles Seeger's *Check-List of Recorded Songs* (some in variant versions).

Transcriptions

1. All the Chickens in the Garden
2. Au Long du Bois
3. Au Pont de l'Anse [37 A2]
4. Auntie Sara in the Bear Grass [420 B2]
5. Cap'n Tom [236 A3]
6. Charles Giteau
7. Claude Allen [1351 A1, or 854 A2]
8. Come here, Dog
9. Daddy Be Gay [1008 A2]
10. Death Have Mercy on My Age [1312 A1]
11. Drop 'em Down [208 A1 or 214 A1]
12. Edward Bold [1006 A2]
13. Erin's Green Shore [1441 A]
14. Glory in the Meetin' House [1536 A2]
15. Grandfather's Dead and Laid under the Ground
16. Hattie Green [211 B2]
17. Hicks' Farewell
18. I Just Stand and Wring My Hands and Cry [711 B1]
19. I'm Goin' to Jine the Army [I'm Going to Join the Army, 1565 A1]
20. It May Be the Last Time [266 B3]
21. Jack Harrold [1344 B2]
22. John de Troy [1401 B]
23. Old Woman under the Hill [1008 A2]
24. The Battle of New Orleans
25. The Black Hills [1852 A2]
26. The Boss of the Section Gang [922 D2]
27. The Bums' Convention in Montreal
28. The Cowgirl [1482 A2]
29. The Cumberland Crew [1605 B1]
30. The Death of Nancy Downing [919 B1]
31. The Drunken Driver [1510 B]

32. The First Day of April [2278 B]
33. The Irish Lady [1717 A2 & B, 1302 B]
34. Windy Bill

Notes

- *Au Long du Bois* and *Au Pont de l'Anse* are not in Seeger's *Check-List,* which contains only English songs.
- *All the Chickens in the Garden* is a children's song, whose provenance is uncertain. The manuscript has the annotation "(Bess sing music to Mrs. Seeger)." There is a version listed in Seeger's *Check-List* (897 B1).
- *The Bums' Convention at Montreal* appears to be from a printed source.
- *The Battle of New Orleans* is from an "old fiddle tune from John B. Jones, Houston, Texas," and includes a page of notes from an article in the *Southern Folk Lore Quarterly,* Sept., 1937. This tune is a distant but recognizable variant of the fiddle tune which bluegrass and old-timey musicians usually call *Eighth of January* (and which, with words written by Jimmie Driftwood, became the popular hit *The Battle of New Orleans* sung by Johnny Horton).
- The manuscript of *Claude Allen* has AFS number 854 A2, and the annotation "Sung by Hillside, Virginia group, Galax, VA., Sept. 1937." This is confusing because 1351 A2 is from Galax, Virginia, 854 A2 from Silverstone, North Carolina.
- The provenance of *Come here, Dog* is uncertain. The first verse is: "Now come here, dog, and get your bone, Tell me what shoulder you want it on."
- *Daddy Be Gay* is listed in Seeger's *Check-List* as *Old Woman under the Hill.*
- The provenance of *Drop 'em Down* is confusing here (as in the main body of the manuscript). AFS number 208 A1 is written on the transcription in the Lomax Family Archives, with the annotation: "Track Horse leader group of Negro convicts singing Huntsville State Penitentiary, Huntsville, Texas." The three entries in Seeger's *Check-List,* for *Drop 'em Down* are 241 A2, 214 A1, and 208 A2 (not A1). The latter is the Mose (Clear Rock) Pratt recording discussed in the endnotes. The following

song in Seeger's *Check-List* (*Drop Old Diamond*, 222 A), however, is sung by Augustus (Track Horse) Haggerty and group in Huntsville, Texas. The lyrics to this transcription of *Drop 'em Down* include the verse:

> Got my diamond blade,
> Drop 'em down,
> Got my diamond blade,
> Drop 'em down.

and

> In the timber,
> heavy loaded,
> Can't you hear me?
> Drop diamond, drop

The above lyrics do not appear in 222 A. Alongside the first verse, in pencil, RCS wrote: "are these words there?" The words "Drop diamond, drop" are circled, and next to them, in pencil, RCS wrote: "Drop 'em diamond?"

- The AFS number of *Grandfather's Dead and Laid under the Ground* is unclear. There are two songs in Seeger's *Check-List* with similar titles, but this one, sung by Sid Jordan, Parchman, Mississippi, 1937, appears to be neither of those.
- The Sacred Harp song, *Hicks' Farewell*, is from a published source.
- *The Irish Lady* is in OSC, as a composite of 1302 B and 1608. The transcription in these manuscripts is very different from the one in OSC.
- The provenance of *Windy Bill* is unclear. It is not even clear that this manuscript is in RCS's hand. An annotation on the bottom mentions that "Patt Patterson of Calif. sent these."
- Some of the songs are listed in Seeger's *Check-List* with slight spelling variants:
  - *Aunty Sarah in the Bear Grass*
  - *I Jus' Wring My Hands and Cry*
  - *I'm Goin' to Join the Army*
  - *Jack Harold*
  - *The Cumberland's Crew*
  - *The Drunken Drivers*

Appendix 3

Amazing Grace/Pisgah Transcription

from George Pullen Jackson, *White and Negro Spirituals*
(New York: J. J. Augustin, 1943)

This unusually elaborate transcription comparing two spirituals is similar to those in *OSC,* but had a more purely analytic intent. It was originally included as a foldout insert at the end of Pullen Jackson's *White and Negro Spirituals* (published just a few years after *OSC;* see Tick, 279), and is currently out of print. Jackson explains and introduces this transcription in his book:

> In Jacksonville I baited the congregation. I asked them to sing for me "Amazing Grace." I had heard white Primitive Baptists sing it at Bildad Church in DeKalb Country, Tennessee, and I knew the song to be a favorite all over the rural Southeast. . . . This would be something to go by, I assured myself. I told Elder Graham I was going to try and sing along.
>
> "That's fine," he agreed, "but I reckon you won't be able to sing it like we do."
>
> And he was right. I started out bravely. I had to hold back. I had to hold long to one note-syllable until they caught up. I "twisted the tune" in my best country manner (which is not very good). They twisted it as I couldn't. But all along I could see that they were singing the old familiar "Amazing Grace" tune as a surge song. I couldn't take down notes. I couldn't ask the congregation to repeat it, even once. So this song got away, too.
>
> The song-catching task which stumped me has been performed

without difficulty by the recording machine. Alan Lomax, Assistant in Charge of the Archive of American Folk Song in the Music Division of the Library of Congress, and his staff have made many recordings of the elusive surge songs and have thus bound them to the analyst's operating table. The song "Amazing Grace" on the sheet inserted at the end of this book, there is transcribed from one of the Archive disks [No. 2684A1, as sung by Jesse Allison and a group of Primitive Baptists in Livingston, Alabama; collected by John A. and Ruby T. Lomax in May, 1939]. It is the text which I had heard in Jacksonville associated with another tune. But what tune was it?

On listening to the record time after time I was struck by the melodic flourish on the word "me" in the middle of the tune, a feature which occurred in only one other tune known to me, the white man's "Pisgah" which is No. 27 in the Tune Comparative List [included at the end of Jackson's book, but in a different key than in RCS's transcription]. . . . On comparison and study of the two tunes I found them to be essentially the same in skeletonic framework from beginning to end.

While the discovery of the "Pisgah" link was mine the detailed transcription of the disc as presented on the insert sheet is the work of Ruth Crawford Seeger. It has been her keen ear, thorough musicianship and friendly co-operation that have made this surge song transcription (the very first one ever brought to notes, I think) one which sets an excellent example for those who may follow in unveiling these monuments of folk art.

"Pisgah" is placed on the top staff of the inserted sheet. The second staff is the skeleton of "Amazing Grace," the Negro surge tune. On the third staff is placed a metrically somewhat simplified form of the surge song which is then transcribed, on the next two staffs, in all detail and with differences as discerned between the men's and the women's singing. The first line-out was not clear on the record. The second stanza is not transcribed, since its differences from the first lie only in unessential details (pp. 249–50).

In this edition, RCS's original hand-written manuscript (which appeared in facsimile in Jackson's book) has been typeset by David Fuqua and myself, with very minor changes.[i]

Editor's Note

i. Notes on this edition of the *Pisgah* transcription:

    1) Near the end, over the text "blind, but," the meter should actually be notated as 17/16 (according to the music): the 8/8 marking is retained (meaning that there is one extra 16th in the measure).

    2) A few cautionary accidentals are inserted (D♯s) under the words "of they" in the two lowest parts.

    3) RCS indicates a meter of 4/4, but the transcription is really in 2/4. The original meter indication is retained.

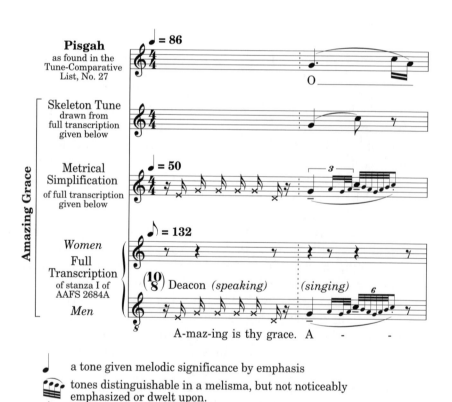

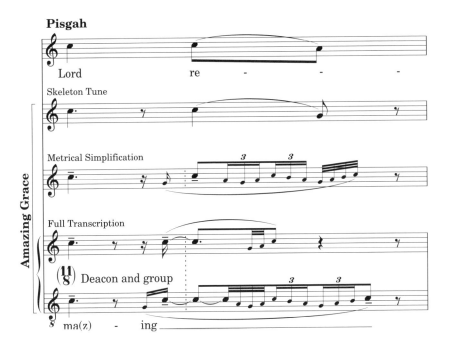

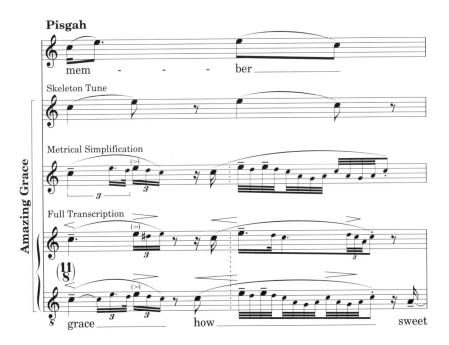

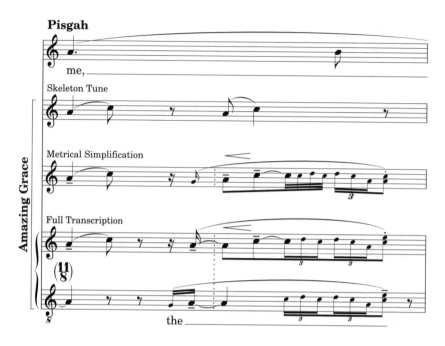

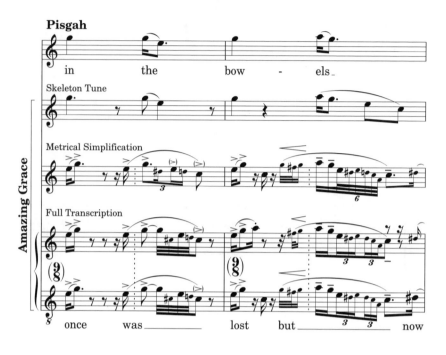

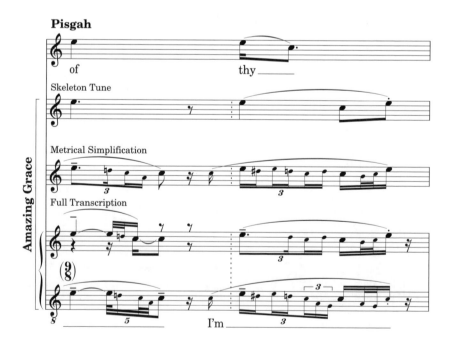

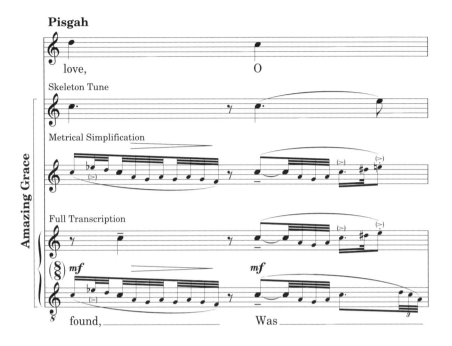

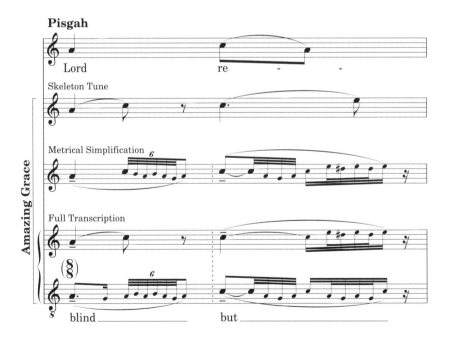

Pisgah

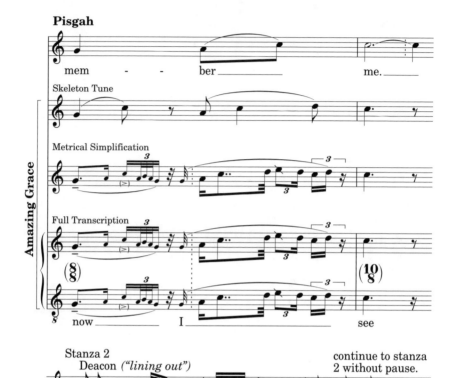

mem - - ber _____ me. _____

Skeleton Tune

Metrical Simplification

Full Transcription

Amazing Grace

now _____ I _____ see

Stanza 2
Deacon *("lining out")*
continue to stanza
2 without pause.

'Twas grace that taught my heart to fear, And grace my fears re-lieved.

Selected Other Writings on American Folk Music

Ruth Crawford Seeger

"Pre-School Children and American Folk Music."
Lecture, later printed in
Matilda Gaume, *Ruth Crawford Seeger: Memoirs, Memories, Music.*
Metuchen, N.J.: Scarecrow Press, 1986.

"Keep the Song Going!"
National Education Association Journal (Feb. 1951): 93–95.

Review of John N. Work, *American Negro Songs for Mixed Voices.*
Notes: Quarterly Journal of the Music Library Association
(December 1948): 172–73.

Editor's Introduction

These three short writings are important scholarly and pedagogical works on folk song by Ruth Crawford Seeger which have not been readily available.

The exact provenance of "Pre-School Children and American Folk Music," as well as the date of its presentation and writing, is uncertain. The manuscript source for this talk is a typescript, with a few pencil indications. It may be a written version of, or notes for, a presentation RCS made to the Music Educator's National Conference in Philadelphia, which involved a group of participating children. Charles Seeger discusses this event and a similar one for television, in "Remembering Ruth Crawford Seeger: An Interview with Charles and Peggy Seeger" (by Ray Wilding-White in *American Music* 6, no. 4 [Winter 1988]: 442–54). Sidney Cowell remembers "a demonstration . . . with a group of children, presented I think for the MENC or some such organization." (Gaume, 114) Gaume cites it as being "not long before her death" (104), and discusses what could be another possible occasion for this talk (113–14): a presentation at the "Shoreham Hotel for the annual Music Teachers National Convention" (but this appears to be in the early 1940s). If the event that Charles Seeger refers to is the occasion for this manuscript, it is almost certainly before 1950. Mike Seeger confirms this (personal conversation), suggesting it is probably from the late 1940s, when she was working on the three books of children's songs. This talk was also published as an appendix in Gaume.

"Keep the Song Going!" and the review of John N. Work's *American Negro Songs for Mixed Voices* are short writings on American folk song in which many of the ideas and philosophies of *The Music of American Folk Song* are applied. Some of "Keep the Song Going!" may consist of the "published version" of the ideas in "Pre-

School Children and American Folk Music" (as in the title itself, which is an important point in the lecture). "Keep the Song Going!" is similar in tone and philosophy to the introductions of RCS's published folk song books for children.

Pre-School Children and American Folk Songs[i]

In a few minutes a dozen four-year-olds will be with us. I am not at all sure what we will be doing. There has been no rehearsing in any distant sense of the word.

It is a question, of course, whether children of this age should be brought before a large group of people, under conditions which might be termed artificial. There is the question of whether it is good for the children.[ii] There is also the question whether those elements which should be uppermost in the bringing of music and children together, can be retained with so many strange faces looking on.

If these children had been subjected in advance to any performance attitudes or disciplines, if they had been drilled or "taught," I would be the first to say certainly No, let's forego whatever values might come to us from having them here.

But what I hope to do this morning is to achieve with the help of the music and the children a complete forgetting on their part of the fact that there is anyone here but themselves and me. I believe we will make that happen (and I beg you to help by refraining from audible appreciation, either through laughter or clapping). What we will do this morning will be what we would do any morning if we were at school.

At school we are too busy with ourselves and the music—with fitting the songs to our thoughts or actions, and fitting our thoughts or actions to the songs—to think much about anyone watching us.[iii] At school we are never sure what will be happening next. No two mornings are ever the same. There is a skeleton plan, of course. Thought is given to balance between active and quiet music, to consistency from day to day, to awareness of weather and the seasons in choices of songs (though if *Jingle Bells* is wanted in June, let's sing it). But plans are really points of departure, to be returned to when

Plate 11. Ruth Crawford Seeger at the Silver Springs Cooperative Nursery School, 1949. (Photo, Seeger family. Used by permission.)
    The little girl in the center with the white shirt and suspenders is Penny Seeger.

needed but often to be stretched and occasionally to be entirely ignored.[iv] If David comes up today with a new idea, we may follow David. If Peter starts kicking his feet up and down in the middle of *Hush Little Baby,* we may even leave the quiet song half finished and let the music pick up the insistent rhythm of Peter's feet. Whether we decide to take such detours depends on a number of things. Does this child need for his own good to be acknowledged as someone who can contribute? Or is he just expressing, a little more vociferously, a group need for action rather than for sustained singing (and how is a teacher to be sure, always, that it is she who is right?)?[v] Or is he perhaps on the edge of becoming a disruptive influence? (And what gives a teacher greater satisfaction than to catch such a moment and help the child and the group to make constructive use of it?)

What we are doing, then, teacher and children, is making something together, fresh each day—a sort of composition. And in any process of composition, large or small, some days are more productive than others. There are valleys and there are high places. The high places are rich with giving and taking between group and teacher. And with giving and taking, the valleys can sometimes reach to high places which are especially satisfying because they promised so little. Certainly if the teacher's first aims are a keen awareness of each child's smallest actions or words or thoughts, and a readiness to follow as well as to lead, there will be a spirit of freshness within the teacher as well as the children, a sense of exploring, of trying something a little new or doing something a little differently. To a tentative basic plan will have been added a vital element: spontaneity.

And if on a platform in conditions unnatural to small children, these qualities can be preserved, surely there must be either in this music or in certain attitudes toward its use, elements which prove themselves to be good for both children and teacher. For the ability to feel comfortable with oneself and with music, even under ordinary circumstances, is a thing we are seeking not only for our children: it is a thing many of us have spent years in seeking for ourselves.

It is my feeling that both these premises are valid. The music itself is American folk music. And this music possesses qualities which invite spontaneity, improvisation, natural participation both in singing and in action. The music itself, therefore—and this means not only the notes and the time values but ways traditional singers and players have of singing and using their music—holds within itself implications as to attitudes toward its use.

Now here come the children. . . .

(A music period with the children follows. Among the songs used are *Mary Wore Her Red Dress, Jim Along Josie, Old Joe Clarke, Hush Little Baby, There Was a Man and He Was Mad, Goodbye Old Paint*. The children leave.)

Before the children came we were speaking of qualities in American folk music and folk performance which are especially good for children—and for the teacher of children. It was through daily using of this music with children[—][vi] and through years of listening to field recordings of it as sung by traditional singers in mountain homes, along roadsides, in fields, churches, towns—that these qualities suggested themselves to me, slowly, one by one. Several of them have been illustrated during the past half hour with the children.

The traditional (folk) singer keeps his song going without interruption of the pulse at stanza ends (though measure lengths may occasionally be irregular). Neither the rhythm nor the mood of the song are broken into by artificial pauses, breaks, ritards, or "expression." This is straightforward music.

Though his tempo is fairly fast, the traditional singer is seldom in a hurry. If he likes a song he will want to sing it over many times. If it has only one stanza, he is likely to sing that stanza over and over without stopping. The children this morning wanted to go on turning around, wanted *Old Joe Clarke* again and again. So we kept it going. At one school a group of four-year-olds kept this up during an entire music period.

Most American traditional music is sung or played with strong rhythmic vitality. Much of it has been used for dancing, for game playing, for work. Children do not need to be urged to let their bodies find ways of moving to music like *Jim Along Josie* or *All Around the Kitchen* or *Old Joe Clarke*.

The traditional singer has not been "taught" this music. He has learned these songs through hearing them. It is my feeling that with small children there should be little or no urging to sing. Mothers of children who sing little or none at school tell me of vigorous and spontaneous singing at home. At school Margie just sat on a stool or stood listening in a corner (and occasionally criticizing) during the three weeks I sang with her group. At the end of the three weeks her mother told me: "We never talk at our house any more. We just sing. Margie won't put on her shoes or button her coat unless we sing about it."

For the teacher there are a number of comforting qualities about this music. It has been thoroughly tested by time and by use—often over generations, and among many people in many places. The teacher can be assured that it is of good quality, yet it [is][vii] also for the most part simple and friendly to learn. She can also be assured that it requires from her no apology for quality of singing voice, that it is accustomed to being sung in a natural way by untrained voices, and is most at home with not too beautiful or polished a tone quality. To the traditional singer it is the song itself which is of value, not the quality of the singer's voice.

Perhaps most important of all, for both children and teacher, is the ease with which these songs can come close to and become part of a child's everyday living. They invite improvisation. To one song new words can be improvised ad lib, and a short song can grow to a very long song. The teacher can, then, know well (i.e., without having to turn the pages of a book) fewer songs—and with fewer songs can fill far greater needs. And the children will be learning tunes as the traditional singer has learned them, naturally, by hearing them and using them, over and over. For this music has grown through being used and being needed, in work, in courting, in religion, in play. It has learned to adapt itself to ever changing environments. It carries, as a result, invaluable comment on the history and customs of the people who have used it. It is a living entity. It is a thing unfinished, not crystallized; a thing to which a child no matter how small or a teacher no matter how hesitant may dare to add some part of himself, thus gaining in even a small way the sort of confidence which can come with making something of one's own. The value he gains for himself in confidence may be out of proportion to the value of his contribution to the song (and the teacher should be sure that the pleasure of adding new words to old songs does not crowd out the older traditional words, which possess values the newer words cannot supplant). But belief in our own worthiness and ability to make our own music is a thing to be nurtured, a thing too often lost early in education. Too early and too frequently music is brought to our attention as something for us to learn. It was made, we are told, by remarkable people like Beethoven and Mozart and Haydn, who when they were young were remarkable children. We are, we feel, not remarkable people. So we say, "I can't" to the making of our own music, and can sense ourselves growing smaller as we say it.

Perhaps feeling comfortable enough and free enough with a song to add their own words to it can be for many children a first step toward feeling free enough with music itself to make their own music. And the "I can" which attends the making of one's own music can be a value as important as food or drink.

Editor's Notes

i. The manuscript of this essay is in the possession of the Seeger family and is used with their permission.

ii. This sentence is omitted from the reprinting of the text in Gaume.

iii. At this point in the source copy, there is a pencilled-in annotation

"AA," with a line leading out towards the left margin. Right before the subsequent sentence "If Peter starts kicking his feet . . ." there is a capital "A" in the left margin, as if this sentence ("If Peter . . .") might have been inserted, in the talk, before "At school. . . ." There is not enough information in the manuscript to argue for reordering the text in this edition.

iv. In the right margin, after the word "ignored" are the pencilled words "To Detours [?] 3." It is unclear what this refers to (or even if that is actually what it says), but, curiously, right before the subsequent word in the text "detours" (a few sentences later) there is a handwritten arrow, pointing downward and to the left. This arrow is handwritten, but appears to be intended as part of the text in some way, as there is an extra space in the typescript between "such" and "detours" which accommodates it.

v. In Gaume, the final question mark is omitted.

vi. The bracketed dash was added by Gaume.

vii. The bracketed word [is] is from Gaume.

Keep the Song Going!ⁱ

We had been singing a song and improvising stanzas about Libby, and color and things to wear.

This la - dy she wears a dark green shawl, a dark green shawl, a dark green shawl, This la - dy she wears a dark green shawl, I love her to my heart.

(From *American Folk Songs for Children,* by Ruth Crawford Seeger [New York: Doubleday, 1948]. Used by permission.)

We kept the song going from one newly made stanza to another, with no pausing between stanzas except for suggestions from Libby. Libby, who is seven, had definite ideas as to what part of herself should come next—her dress, socks, bracelet, shoes, hair, even her "sun-tan skin."

"This Libby she wears her sun-tan skin,
Her sun-tan skin, her sun-tan skin,
This Libby she wears her sun-tan skin,
I love her to my heart."

When at last the song stopped, she said, "Now I'm all clothed with a song." Maybe Libby expressed the satisfaction children feel as they take hold of a song, sing anywhere from one to a dozen of its traditional stanzas, and then make up a dozen more of their own.

In my work with music and children, I have sung in schools with groups of varying ages from nursery thru elementary-school age and beyond—not to mention parents, who also like to sing. In the several schools whose music programs have been under my direction, we have sung for the most part American traditional music. Singing sessions with each grade or group were usually two or three a week.

Improvisation on the words of songs was a part of each group's experience—with the younger grades, a large part; with the older grades, relatively less, but never ignored. It was something we all liked to do.

Comfortable with the Song

There is a feeling among a group which contains something special when the last of the printed words has been sung, and yet the music keeps on going back to the beginning for another stanza—impelling the group to provide more words.

During that process of giving the song reason for continuing, the group and the song seem to come close enough to each other to touch. The group has given to the song, and the song has given to the group. Such exchange makes for good friendship. It is certainly a step toward getting acquainted, toward feeling comfortable with a thing or a person.

During the process of keeping a song going thru word improvisation—of becoming wrapped or clothed with a song—the emphasis is on content rather than technic, on the song itself rather than on the learning of the song. It's "let's sing" rather than "let's learn." Attention is directed more toward word content than toward music content. The tune is being used as a sort of clothesline on whose curves are to be hung a variety of changing words and thoughts.

The third grade is singing its current favorite, *Paper of Pins.* We sing all the traditional stanzas we know, for the flavor of the old traditional words is an essential part of a folk song. Then, with no more stanzas to sing, the song still keeps going, begins again. "Oh, I will give you. . ." and stops in mid-air, waiting for words.

Ideas come fast. Here's a hand waving, and another, and plenty more. It's hard making them wait their turn, and only a matter of choosing from among them—"Oh, I will give you an aeroplane."

Now there are more hands than before. And again we choose, and sing the newly made stanza with a pleasure that is almost a pleasure of tasting.

> "Oh, I will give you an aeroplane
> That you may ride from Maine to Spain,
> If you will marry me, me, me,
> If you will marry me."

And the process continues, for as long as everybody wants the song to keep going.

> "Oh, I will give you a house of bricks
> For cement I'll use some pancake mix."

> "Oh, I will give you a washing machine
> That you may wash my clothes so clean."

And on to clocks and books and desks. . . .

There is nothing new about the idea of feeling comfortable enough with a song to make up new words, lines, or stanzas to it. Folk songs have been treated with that sort of informality for a long time. Without it, many of the traditional songs we like best would not have been learned and passed on from one generation to another.

Singing-games, dance songs, love songs, courting songs, nonsense songs, work songs, and spiritual songs have grown and been kept living by means of a long-term process of improvisation and give-and-take. This process is, in character, not unlike one of these little group sessions of ours—a process which may have stretched over 20 years or 50 or 100 or 200, rather than a brief 20 to 40 minutes.

The many traditional stanzas of a song are a patchwork quilt made by generations of singers. Perhaps it is partly because folk music has grown in this manner and has been used in so many different ways, that children (and teachers and parents) feel especially at home with it—*and find it easy to learn.*

Somewhere along the way during such a session of word improvisation, most of the children in the group have absorbed the tune. The repetition which contributes to the learning of a tune has taken place naturally and pleasurably. And the process of thinking up new words or lines which can be sung with the tune has automatically given the children a sense of the song's contours and rhythms.

Improvising new words to a song helps children toward feeling comfortable with music, because they are themselves being active about the song. They are doing something with it; they are treating the song as a thing which can change and develop, like themselves. It has been presented to them not as a thing perfect and inevitably finished, but as a thing which can never be finished.

A song unfinished is a little like a fine charm bracelet such as children wear: a tune and a stanza or two to start with, plenty of chance to add more as time goes on.

Comfortable Within and Without

Improvising words to a song not only helps a group of children to feel comfortable with the music. It helps them feel more comfortable with each other. They have been making something together. They have had a taste, however minute, of creating—of communal composing. The pleasure in this small achievement can be measured by the gusto with which the children sing the stanzas they have made.

A child who feels comfortable with other children is usually progressing in the large job of feeling comfortable with himself—a project which probably occupies much of his endeavor during most of his day. If music can make even a small contribution to this task, it will have given a child a thing of great value to himself and to others who are touched by his thoughts or actions.

Feeling comfortable with himself involves, or course, feeling confidence in himself. We are all acquainted with the inner tension which expresses itself in the words "I can't." You can almost see a child's picture of himself growing smaller as he says the words. Many children, especially when they get to be of school age, have come to think they can't make up their own music. Music has been made up by great musicians who were remarkable when they were children (all the books say so).

But you use words every day. You make up your own way of telling what happened on the way to school. So why not go a little farther and dare to make up words to someone else's tune? Word improvisation, then, tho not in itself a direct musically creative process, can conceivably be a freeing step toward it.

The Teacher Feels Comfortable, Too

Of course, to help children toward feeling comfortable with music, the teacher must be comfortable with it.

Toward fine-art ("classical" or composed) music, it is inevitable that we feel a certain weight of responsibility. Folk music, on the other hand, carries few constraining traditions of performance. Emphasis is on straightforwardness rather than variety in manner of performance.

The folk-singer's attention is centered on the song rather than on the manner in which he is singing it. He feels no apology, no undue pride, for the quality of his voice. Except when singing story-telling songs like ballads, he need have no worry about forgetting words or stanzas: he can always make them up on the spot, or someone else can make them.

The teacher can feel comfortable with this kind of music. She can sing, as folk singers do, with no sense of apology for a natural untrained voice. She can feel free, as folk singers do, to sing without an instrument (tho if she plays a guitar, ukelele, banjo, auto-harp—or a piano—she should certainly make use of it). She and the children can join in the pleasure of giving attention to the song itself, secure in the assurance that this music should be sung *not* too carefully, too smoothly, too "beautifully."

And she can meet a greater number of needs with fewer songs. Rather than spend her time half learning a large number of songs, she can, in the same amount of time, make thoro[ii] acquaintance with a moderate number. She can bring these to the children with unhurried confidence because she knows them well. She can use them at the moment she needs them.

A Bit of Magic

A morning at a recent children's book fair provides illustration. Another speaker and I discovered that we were sharing between us a succession of 15–minute periods, with groups of a hundred or so children at each period, ranging in age from five to 12. To some groups, the speaker told a story about deep-sea diving; to others, a story about beetles and their relative light and dark shades in caves and above ground.

When she turned to me suggesting a song about beetles or fish, she struck a weak point in my repertory. But there is a rabbit song which our family is fond of. So I suggested to the children that morning that we try a bit of magic—take a rabbit and turn it into a beetle or a fish.

First, we gained singing acquaintance with the song thru several of its traditional rabbit stanzas. Then, we proceeded to more stanzas of our own making about fish and beetles. And the flow of newly made stanzas was interrupted only by the coming and going of the children.

We Can Carry It So Far

A few warnings should be borne in mind as we enjoy with children the making of new words to songs. The teacher, finding that making up stanzas is fun, will need to guard against contributing too many ideas herself. She should let the children do most if not all of the giving. Her suggestions will seldom be necessary, and are likely to be more literary, less natural, and less in the spirit of folk tradition.

The teacher must also be sure to give the children continued experience with the traditional words, no matter how much improvising fun the children are having with a song. The traditional words have values which the newer words do not have. The old and the new are both essential to the song's staying alive and growing; the new should contribute to the old, but should not supplant it. If the new is allowed to crowd out the old, the identity of the song may suffer or be lost.

Perhaps, we might compare improvising a song with a passenger train—the tune as the engine and the stanzas as cars. You can add any number of coaches of different kinds. You can even add a few freight cars. But if too many freight cars are added, the passenger train becomes a freight train—with quite a different character, and probably with a different destination.

Editor's Notes

i. National Education Association Journal (February, 1951): 93–95. This article was accompanied by the short biographical note: "Mrs. Seeger is a teacher in Chevy Chase, Maryland. She is author of *American Folk Songs for Children* and *Animal Folk Songs for Children*." Reprinted by permission of the National Education Association.

ii. "Thoro" (as well as the words "tho" and "thru") in the original, are left as is.

[Review of][i] John N. Work, Composer and Arranger, *American Negro Songs for Mixed Voices* (Philadelphia: Theodore Presser Co., 1948, 259 pp., $1.50)

This collection is obviously a re-publication from the same plates as the 1940 edition published under the same title by Howell, Soskin, and Company,[ii] and it is therefore already a well-known contribution. Since, however, it has not been reviewed in these pages, and since its re-publication by a music publisher gives this outstanding collection now to a new and undoubtedly wider, singing public, an evaluation eight years later is not out of order.

The initial five chapters preceding the 230 songs are of distinct value, with the first two of special significance: *Origins, The Spiritual, The Blues, Work Songs,* and *Social and Miscellaneous Songs.* The songs themselves are for the most part spiritual songs, with a few fine work songs at the end, a few social songs, and a scattering of three-phrase songs suggesting blues relationship. In full appreciation of the fact that many spiritual songs and work songs have common roots, I venture to suggest that a more accurate title, indicating the preponderance of the spiritual songs, might have been found.

Mr. Work ably enters the discussion carried on these past fifteen years concerning the Negro versus white origins in Negro spiritual songs. The points he makes are well taken. It has seemed to me for some time that claims for preponderance of white origin in Negro spiritual music have laid too great weight on the importance of tonal skeleton and the written source, and too little on the rhythmic and tonal flesh in which the skeleton is clothed by the rich and varied singing style of this oral tradition. Also given too little consideration is the fact that in any creative process, either in fine art or folk music, the utilization of materials already current in the tradition is to be taken for granted; that any live tradition, fine art or folk, lives by means of a process such as Mr. Work terms "re-assembling" (I prefer "re-composing"); and that as Mr. Work points out there is a big difference between this process and "imitation." Certainly, the Negro seized upon elements that were vital in the European-American tradition with which he found himself surrounded. Certainly, too, he contributed elements that were vital and had survived in his own tradition. Essential to the evaluation of the product of a folk singer as well as of a Beethoven, however, is the question of what elements in the inherited tradition were considered by him vital enough to be chosen as the warp into which to weave his own unique contribution.

Mr. Work occasionally weakens his own argument by apology for characteristics in Negro song which might be said to comprise strength rather than weakness. He tends to explain away some "incongruous materials" and differences in manner of singing as the result of inaccurate remembering or of individual idiosyncracy not yet ironed out by group use, whereas it is a question whether such "inaccurate reproduction" might not better be constructively valued and praised, in most cases, as partaking of the nature of re-composition. The ruggedness of "imperfect," unsmoothed-out versions, of "unnatural intervals," or "words that do not quite fit the meter" are things greatly to be valued in any folk music.

Further inconsistency is frequently shown in the harmonizations of the songs, which belong much more to typical vertical four-part written hymnal tradition of the late nineteenth century than to the free, barer, more linear manner of group singing of which such settings as *Sittin' down by the Side of the Lamb, My Soul's been Anchored in the Lord,* and *Hammering* are fine examples. Credit should be given Mr. Work, however, for including so many of these sparer settings. Also, attention should be called in one breath to admirable omission of fancy secondary triads and sevenths, but on the other hand to over-use of the typically fine art tonic 6/4 chord, and to the still greater overuse of the final cadence V^7—I, which occurs in a good three-quarters of the 175 four-part settings.

There is a wealth of fine, down-swooping melodic line in the book in songs like *Hammering, Calvary, The Angels Done Bowed Down, I Never Felt Such Love in my Soul befo'*, and *Come here Lord*. There are numerous songs which exhibit the lowered 3rd and 7th degrees of the scale, and a few showing less customary tonal departures, such as the raised 4th in *I am the True Vine*. There are haunting melodies like that of *Shepherd, Shepherd*, whose "unusual" interval sequence almost obscures, at first, its relationship with *Sometimes I feel like a Motherless Child*. Special praise also goes to the goodly number of melodic transcriptions like *Jesus goin' to Make up my Dying Bed*, with tonal slides helping the reader to a sense of singing style. In fact, Mr. Work has achieved a balance not easy to attain in presenting so much of singing style, tonally and rhythmically, without making the songs too difficult for the average reader to use and enjoy.

Everything considered, this is a book which should be in the hands not only of those whose special field lies in traditional American music but of group music teachers of children large and small, and of leaders of group singing.

Editor's Notes

i. Reprinted from *Notes: Quarterly Journal of the Music Library Association* 6, no. 1 (December 1948) by permission of the Music Library Association.

ii. There was another edition of this book in 1940, published in New York by Crown. Various reprints have had slightly differing titles from the 1940 Howell, Soskin edition.

Index of Songs

Song titles in italics are mentioned in the book, but not in Ruth Crawford Seeger's *The Music of American Folk Song.*

Index

This is the first publication of an annotated monograph by the noted composer and folksong scholar Ruth Crawford Seeger. Originally written as a foreword for the 1940 book *Our Singing Country,* it was considered too long and was replaced by a much shorter version. According to her stepson, Pete Seeger, when the original was not included "Ruth suffered one of the biggest disappointments of the last ten years of her life. It just killed her . . . She was trying to analyze the whole style and problem of performing this music." Along with her children Mike and Peggy Seeger, he has long desired to see this work in print as it was meant to be read.

The manuscript has been edited from several varying sources by Larry Polansky, with the assistance of Seeger's biographer Judith Tick. It is divided into two sections: I. 'A Note on Transcription' and II. 'Notes on the Songs and on Manners of Singing.' Seeger examines all aspects of the relationship between singer, song, notation, the eventual performer, and the transcriber. Her approach foreshadowed a great deal of contemporary ethnomusicological thought.

In Section I, Seeger develops a complex and well-organized system of notation for these songs which is meant to be both descriptive (transcription as cultural preservation) and prescriptive (she intended that others would be able to perform these songs). In Section II, she provides an interpretive theory for performance of this music, and suggests how performers might make the songs 'their own' through a deep knowledge of the original styles.

Ruth Crawford Seeger considered this work to be both a major accomplishment and a central statement of her own ideas on the topic. The University of Rochester Press is proud to make it available as she wished.

Larry Polansky is the Strauss Professor of Music at Dartmouth College, and a well-known composer, theorist, performer and American music scholar.

Judith Tick is Matthews Distinguished University Professor, Department of Music at Northeastern University and author of *Ruth Crawford Seeger: A Composer's Search for American Music* (1997).